The Ignatian Adventure

THE IGNATIAN ADVENTURE

Experiencing the Spiritual Exercises
of Saint Ignatius in Daily Life

KEVIN O'BRIEN, SJ

LOYOLA PRESS.
A JESUIT MINISTRY
Chicago

LOYOLA PRESS.
A JESUIT MINISTRY

3441 N. Ashland Avenue
Chicago, Illinois 60657
(800) 621-1008
www.loyolapress.com

Imprimi potest: Very Rev. James Shea, SJ, Provincial.

Scripture quotations contained herein are from the New Revised Standard Version Bible: Catholic Edition, copyright 1993 and 1989 by the Division of Christian Education of the National Council of the Churches of Christ in the U.S.A. Used by permission. All rights reserved.

Unless otherwise noted, all quotations from The Spiritual Exercises are taken from *The Spiritual Exercises of Saint Ignatius: A Translation and Commentary by George E. Ganss, S.J.* (St. Louis: The Institute of Jesuit Sources, 1992). Used by permission.

The poems "Messenger" on p. 47 and "Praying" on p. 73 are from *Thirst* by Mary Oliver. Copyright © 2006 by Mary Oliver. Reprinted by permission of Beacon Press, Boston.

Cover image: © iStockphoto.com/olaser

Library of Congress Cataloging-in-Publication Data
O'Brien, Kevin F.
  The Ignatian adventure : the Spiritual exercises of Saint Ignatius in daily life / Kevin F. O'Brien.
    p. cm.
  Includes bibliographical references.
  ISBN-13: 978-0-8294-3577-1
  ISBN-10: 0-8294-3577-8
1. Ignatius, of Loyola, Saint, 1491-1556. Exercitia spiritualia. 2. Spiritual exercises. 3. Spiritual direction. 4. Spiritual life—Catholic Church. I. Title.
  BX2179.L8O26 2011
  248.3—dc23
                                                                    2011019551

Printed in the United States of America
    19 20 21 22 23 24 Bang 14 13 12 11 10 9 8

For Mom, Dad, Cathy, and Andy,
and for my family in the Society of Jesus

Ad Majorem Dei Gloriam
"For the Greater Glory of God"

CONTENTS

Beginning   1

The Journey of Ignatius of Loyola   5

The Ignatian Adventure   13

Different Paths, Same Journey   19

Preparing for the Adventure   23

A Note to Spiritual Directors and Retreat Leaders   29

The Adventure Begins: Encountering the
Unconditional, Creative, Inviting Love of God   31

Week of Prayer #1: God's Unconditional Love for Me   38

The "Presupposition" of the Spiritual Exercises   43

Week of Prayer #2: God's Ongoing Creation   45

Week of Prayer #3: The Intimacy of Prayer   49

Distractions in Prayer   53

Images of God   55

Week of Prayer #4: God's Invitation to Greater Freedom   57

Ignatian Repetition   61

Week of Prayer #5: The Principle and Foundation   63

Principle and Foundation: Traditional Translation   67

Principle and Foundation: Contemporary Translation   69

Week of Prayer #6: God's Call to Me   71

St. Ignatius's Prayer of Awareness: The Examen   75

The "First Week": Experiencing the Boundless
Mercy of God   79

Week of Prayer #7: The Reality of Sin   90

The Colloquy   95

Week of Prayer #8: My Own History of Sin and Grace   97

Week of Prayer #9: The Causes and Consequences of Sin 102

Experiences of Boredom or Dryness in Prayer   109

Week of Prayer #10: God's Merciful Love for Me   112

Introduction to the Discernment of Spirits   115

The "Second Week": Accompanying Jesus Christ
on Mission   119

Week of Prayer #11: The Contemplation on the
Incarnation   129

Gentle Reminders   135

Week of Prayer #12: The Birth of Jesus   137

Ignatian Contemplation: Imaginative Prayer   141

Week of Prayer #13: The Childhood of Jesus   143

Rules for Discernment of Spirits: How the Good
Spirit and Evil Spirit Operate   145

Week of Prayer #14: The Hidden Life of Jesus   147

Rules for Discernment of Spirits: Storing Up the Graces
of Consolation   151

Week of Prayer #15: The Call of Christ, Our King   153

Poverty of Spirit   159

Week of Prayer #16: Jesus' Public Ministry Begins   162

Rules for Discernment of Spirits: Dealing with
Spiritual Desolation   165

Week of Prayer #17: Meditation on Two Standards   168

Week of Prayer #18: The Call and Cost of Discipleship   176

Rules for Discernment of Spirits: Reasons We
Experience Desolation   181

Week of Prayer #19: Three Ways of Loving   183

Week of Prayer #20: Jesus' Public Ministry   188

Rules for Discernment of Spirits: Three Metaphors for
How the Enemy Acts in Our Lives   191

Week of Prayer #21: The Kingdom of God   196

Week of Prayer #22: Jesus as Human and Divine   200

The Election: *Spiritual Exercises* 169–189   203

The "Third Week": Being with Jesus in His Suffering
and Savoring the Grace of Compassion   209

Week of Prayer #23: The Road to Calvary   216

Rules for Discernment of Spirits: Distinguishing Between
Authentic and False Spiritual Consolation   219

Week of Prayer #24: The Arrest of Jesus   222

Rules for Discernment of Spirits: Discovering False
Spiritual Consolation   225

Week of Prayer #25: The Suffering and Death of Jesus   227

Week of Prayer #26: The Paschal Mystery   230

The "Fourth Week": Experiencing the Joy and
Sharing the Consolation of the Risen Lord   233

Week of Prayer #27: The Resurrection of Jesus Christ   240

Week of Prayer #28: The Risen Life   244

Week of Prayer #29: The Contemplation of the
Love of God   248

Week of Prayer #30: Life in the Spirit   256

Week of Prayer #31: Gathering the Graces   259

Week of Prayer #32: Looking Ahead with Hope   262

An Adventure Continues   265

Living the Spiritual Exercises   269

In Gratitude   273

Acknowledgments   275

Sources   277

Spiritual Resources for the Journey of Faith   283

Beginning

EVERY ADVENTURE HAS A BEGINNING. Great adventures often have the most unexpected beginnings. For me, the adventure that would lead me to become a Jesuit and to write this guide to prayer began on a hot day outside a courthouse in southern Florida, in the company of an eighty-year-old Jewish woman from Brooklyn.

I was a junior lawyer working on a big probate case involving some tragic family history and lots of land in Palm Beach County. The stakes were high, and the facts were deeply personal for my client, Miriam. She was immensely kind and gracious. At this stage of her life, the last place she wanted to be was in a courtroom, in a long, drawn-out fight over a will. But she knew that it was the right thing to do for her beloved, whose will we were trying to defend.

As the junior lawyer, my job mostly was to care for the personal needs of the client. During the court hearings recounting some of the painful family history, Miriam sometimes would leave the courtroom, and I would walk with her. She would tell me stories about her beloved and about growing up in Brooklyn. She would tell me about her hopes for her future. One day, as we walked outside the courthouse, the sun beating down on us, it hit me: *I would rather be outside talking with Miriam than inside the courtroom.* There was no blinding light, no thunderbolt from heaven, just an insight that cut to the heart of the matter.

The thought was not entirely new. I went to law school not intending to practice law but to lay the foundation for a career in politics. From an early age, my family and my faith taught me that, whatever I did in life, I needed to give back to the community. The gospel truth became a part of me; to whom much is given, much is expected. Tied up in this noble ambition was a lot of youthful ambition. Admittedly, public service fed my ego and my desire for power and prestige. But God works with our mixed motivations, refining ambitions that are too self-directed.

So I knew that practicing law would not be for the long term. What I did not know then was that my way of serving and giving back would be as a Jesuit priest, not as a public servant. Raised in an Irish Catholic family, with twelve years of Catholic education behind me, I had at times thought about becoming a priest, most seriously while at Georgetown, where I attended college. But my interest in the Jesuits then was more about my esteem for the Jesuits I met there than about a personal sense of calling. In short, lots of seeds had been planted earlier in my life; they just needed the proper watering.

That day with Miriam outside the courthouse was a moment when my patient and gently persistent God broke through my cluttered thinking and clearly got my attention. What that insight did was stir up a visceral gut check in me. I needed to pay attention and figure out what I really wanted to do with my life, concerns that are common among twenty-six-year-olds, like myself then. I talked more pointedly with friends and mentors who knew me well; I started to pray more regularly, inviting God into the conversation about what I should do with my life. Thoughts about becoming a priest reemerged naturally.

The lawyer in me wanted to figure it out quickly and cut to the chase. So I approached a seasoned spiritual director and matter-of-factly (and somewhat arrogantly) stated, "I'd like for you to help me figure out if I should be a Jesuit priest." She astutely put me in my place, saying to me in her Irish brogue, "Well, now, let's put that question aside for a time. Tell me, who is God for you?" I was at a loss for words. We spent about a year trying to come up with an answer to that initial, and crucial, question.

God has a way of getting our attention and sending the right people to us at the right times. The problem is that we often don't realize it at the moment. Fortunately, I was picking up on God's cues. About the same time as my graced conversation with Miriam, I was talking with the principal of our local Catholic high school and my alma mater, Cardinal Newman High School, in West Palm Beach. After an advisory board meeting one evening, Colleen, who had known me as a student some years before, asked me, "Have you ever thought about teaching?" The truth was that I had thought about teaching over the years, having tutored in college and served as a teaching assistant in law school. But my initial answer was the expected one: "Thanks, that's very kind, but I'm developing a law practice and I'm building this career in politics, and . . ."

Coupled with my insight outside the courthouse, Colleen's question continued to intrigue me. Within a few weeks, I accepted her offer. Whenever I thought about teaching, I experienced a deep-seated enthusiasm, and my imagination was stirred with all sorts of possibilities. Practicing law, though a good and noble profession, did not summon the same bold, deep desires. The partners at my law firm offered, "Take a year off. We'll save a place for you." Some thought I'd come back. Those who knew me best realized I was beginning another adventure that would take me away from the practice of law.

For three years, I taught history, political science, economics, and religion at Cardinal Newman. I coached girls' soccer. I started a retreat program. I loved it. I found a passion and a joy in my work that I had not experienced anywhere else. I felt alive, and the people around me saw that. The environment of the high school was fertile ground for my consideration of a vocation to the priesthood. My work and my students helped me realize my vocation as a priest, and the most natural place for me to live that priesthood was as a Jesuit.

The Jesuits whom I had known were talented, energetic, smart, funny, committed men. They lived joy-filled lives. They preached, taught, and discussed the loftiest and most inspiring ideas, yet they also lived very much with their feet firmly set on the ground. They practiced a spirituality that was deeply rooted in the world, finding God in all things, meeting people right where they were, and responding to the most pressing needs of our time. They committed themselves to a faith that does justice, caring and advocating for the most vulnerable people in our world. They did not hesitate to go to the frontiers where the church meets the world and the world meets the church, bringing the gospel to new conversations and environments in a variety of cultures and religions.

The Jesuits were men of passion. They promised me a life of adventure, not simply of the geographic kind (I *have* moved around a lot) but one leading me to the most important destination of all: to the heart of God, which fills the hearts of all people. My guidebook in this great adventure has been the Spiritual Exercises of St. Ignatius, which is what this book is all about. The genius and beauty of the Exercises is that we learn to weave our own life narrative into the life story of Jesus Christ in such a way that both become more vivid and interconnected. The Spiritual Exercises have helped me become more aware of how God has guided me in the past, how God labors in my life in the present and calls me in the future. The Exercises do this by helping me become freer of all the interior clutter that gets in the way of reaching this graced awareness.

There is another story that animates the Exercises but that never gets in the way of the more important encounter between the person and Jesus Christ. It is the story of Ignatius of Loyola, who will serve as our able guide, pointing us in the right direction and equipping us with what we need for the journey. As a young man, Ignatius dreamed of a life of adventure. Along the way, he crafted the Exercises as a testament of grace, a record of his own encounter with the living God, which he shared with more and more people. His adventure had a beginning—and like all great adventures, its beginning was most unexpected.

The Journey of Ignatius of Loyola

Iñigo López de Loyola y Oñaz was born in 1491, the thirteenth child in a family of minor nobility. Like other boys coming of age at that time, Iñigo imagined himself as one of the knights he read about in the romantic novels of his era: cultured, pious, skilled in warfare, and irresistible to ladies-in-waiting.

The times fermented the idealism and passion that were in his Basque blood. It was an age for adventurers of all kinds: merchants crisscrossing continents and seas in search of new wealth; explorers setting out on expeditions to unknown worlds; writers, artists, and scientists inspiring a rebirth in learning that would expand the reaches of the mind and culture. In his youth, Iñigo could not have imagined the very different kind of adventure that God had in store for him.

The Young Knight

Iñigo's family connections helped secure him a position serving as a page to the treasurer of the kingdom of Castile. So he left his native Loyola at the age of sixteen for a life at court. The upwardly mobile Iñigo easily fit into his new role: riding, dueling, gambling, dancing, and romancing young ladies. Though short in stature, he got involved in some noteworthy brawls, one of which resulted in charges being filed against him.

When he was twenty-six, Iñigo took up the life of a soldier in the northern town of Pamplona. Ever loyal, Iñigo did not hesitate to come to the Crown's defense when in 1521 the French attacked Pamplona. It was a lost battle from the start, with Iñigo's small band of soldiers easily outnumbered. As a matter of honor, Iñigo refused to give up the town fortress. Through the walls of the citadel crashed a cannonball, which struck Iñigo in the legs. Impressed by Iñigo's courage, the French soldiers tended to his wounds and carried him back to Loyola, where doctors reset his legs. He almost died from an infection related to the injury.

As with his loyalty and honor, Iñigo's vanity ran deep. After his legs were rebroken and had begun to heal, he noticed that his right leg was shorter than his left and that there was an unsightly protrusion of the bone. He worried that these deformities would spell the end of his knightly life. He fretted over not being able to wear the flashy, tight-fitting clothing of a courtier. So he had his doctors break and reset his limb again, saw off the bump on his leg, and stretch his shorter leg in a racklike instrument. The pain was excruciating but, in his worldly estimation, worth it.

For six months, the restless Iñigo convalesced. To pass the time, he asked his caregiver for some novels of chivalry to read, but all she could find were a popular version of the life of Christ and a collection of tales of saints. As he read and pondered these books, he noticed a change taking place within him. Daydreams of serving the king as a valiant knight and winning the love of a noble lady, though at first enticing, ultimately left him feeling inwardly dry and discontented. By contrast, when he imagined devoting his life to the service of God and others, as had the saints he was reading about, Iñigo experienced a deep sense of joy. In his autobiography, written in the third person and dictated to a fellow Jesuit near the end of his life, Ignatius writes:

> When he thought of worldly matters, he found much delight; but after growing weary and dismissing them, he found that he was dry and unhappy. But when he thought of . . . imitating the saints in all the austerities they practiced, he not only found consolation in

these thoughts, but even after they had left him he remained happy and joyful. (*Autobiography*, no. 8)

God was stirring up something new in our young knight. Ignatius became convinced that God was speaking to him through his interior attractions and reactions.

The Pilgrim

Iñigo wisely wanted to test what these unfamiliar desires and dreams were all about. So once he recovered from his injuries, he set out on a new adventure, intending to go to Jerusalem as a pilgrim. He left behind his stately family home and traveled widely—begging, preaching, and caring for the sick and poor. One of his first stops was a Benedictine mountaintop shrine of Our Lady at Montserrat. There, after an all-night vigil, the young romantic left behind his sword before the altar of Our Lady and donned the sackcloth of a beggar. With a pilgrim's staff in hand, Iñigo gave his courtly robe and feathered cap to a beggar.

From Montserrat he set out for the small town of Manresa. Iñigo stayed there for about ten months, spending hours every day in solitary prayer and working at a hospice. Later in his life, he reflected that during this time, God worked on him like a teacher instructing a student, gently schooling him in the ways of prayer and holiness. At Manresa, Iñigo discerned carefully the interior movements of his soul: the attractions, feelings, thoughts, and desires that led him to greater intimacy with Jesus Christ and those that were distractions to his spiritual growth. Trying to outdo the piety of the saints he read about, he engaged in severe bodily penances. At times, he became mired in self-doubt. Through prayer and wise spiritual guidance, Iñigo discerned that his seemingly pious acts were really displays of vanity. As he sought a more balanced spiritual life, he encountered a God who was not a tyrant waiting for him to slip up but a helping God who wanted for him the fullness of life.

At Manresa, Iñigo enjoyed the first of several mystical visions that would mark his life. Sitting by the river Cardoner, he experienced an enlightenment that allowed him to see the world with new eyes and to find God in all things. In his autobiography, the pilgrim saint remarked that he learned more about God and the world in that one moment than he did throughout the rest of his life.

Iñigo began to make notes of his spiritual insights. He talked to people about the spiritual life whenever and wherever he could and recorded the fruit of these conversations. Those notes became the basis for a manual of prayer that he would later title the *Spiritual Exercises*.

The pilgrim begged his way to Jerusalem in 1523. Iñigo intended to spend the rest of his life in the region where Jesus had lived and labored. However, because of the dangerous political situation in the Holy Land at the time, the Franciscan guardians of the sacred sites ordered him to leave after only a few weeks. His romantic hopes of spending his life in the Holy Land dashed, Iñigo faced a moment of decision: how was he to serve God? He writes, again in the third person:

> After the said pilgrim came to realize that it was God's will that he not remain in Jerusalem, he kept wondering what he ought to do, and finally he was inclined toward spending some time in studies in order to help souls; and so he decided to go to Barcelona. (*Autobiography*, no. 50)

Underlying this succinct, matter-of-fact account are some profound spiritual insights. Iñigo was learning that he had to be flexible in responding to God's will in his life. And his decisions had to be directed toward "helping souls," or helping people, which he could do in many ways, all depending on the circumstances he faced.

The Student

Once back in Spain, Iñigo decided to begin studies for the priesthood, but he lacked knowledge of Latin, the language of the church. So at the age of thirty-three, he spent two years in Barcelona, studying alongside schoolchildren. Iñigo subsequently attended universities in Alcalá and Salamanca, but his education was self-directed and haphazard. In these university towns, he continued to preach, teach, and offer his Spiritual Exercises. He was arrested several times by the Spanish Inquisition, which questioned his credentials and carefully examined the Spiritual Exercises for heresy. The authorities limited Iñigo's ability to teach and preach, but they did not condemn the Spiritual Exercises.

Lacking formal academic training and wanting to become a better teacher and preacher, Iñigo traveled to the renowned University of Paris to study philosophy and theology. There he became known as "Ignatius," a Latin form of his name. In Paris, he met other students, such as Francis Xavier and Peter Faber, who were captivated by Ignatius's experience of God, his vision of the world, and his adventurous spirit.

On August 15, 1534, in a small chapel on Montmartre, the "hill of martyrs," in Paris, Ignatius and six other men professed religious vows of poverty and chastity to bind them more closely together. They also vowed to travel to the Holy Land after completing their studies for the priesthood. If, after a year, passage proved impractical, they promised to offer their services to the pope instead.

The Founder

The companions, now eleven in number, met in Venice and preached, worked in hospitals, and gave the Exercises. While waiting for passage to Jerusalem, Ignatius and those others who were not yet priests were ordained in 1537. Unable to go to the Holy

Land because Venice was at war with the Ottoman Empire, these "friends in the Lord," as they called themselves, set out for Rome as they had vowed.

Along the way, near Rome, in a chapel in the small village of La Storta, Ignatius enjoyed another mystical vision, in which he saw God the Father with Jesus, the Son, carrying his cross. Ignatius heard the Father say, "I will be favorable to you in Rome." In the vision, Ignatius had a clear sense of being called to serve alongside Jesus.

When they settled in Rome, the companions deliberated for many weeks about their future, all the while teaching, preaching, and performing works of mercy. They eventually decided to form a religious order under a vow of obedience to a superior. Ignatius was their unanimous choice.

Inspired by the vision at La Storta, Ignatius insisted that they call themselves the Company (or Society) of Jesus. They dared to take the name of Jesus (which no other religious order had done) for the simple reason that knowing, loving, and serving Jesus Christ was the inspiration and end of their mission together. They wanted to be companions of Jesus carrying his cross.

The Jesuits, as the companions soon would be called, vowed to go wherever the church's needs were greatest and wherever they could help more souls. Unlike monastic religious orders, their home would be the road. The Jesuits would meet people where they were rather than insist that people come to a monastery or a church. They offered the church a spirituality that was both mystical and practical; they would be "contemplatives in action," as the first generation of Jesuits described themselves.

When their religious order was formally constituted in 1540, the pope began to depend on the Jesuits for important missions throughout the world. Xavier set sail for India. Faber and his fellow theologians were assigned to participate in the Council of Trent. Jesuits opened schools all over Europe and across the seas to meet the church's great desire for an educated clergy and faithful. Ignatius and his Jesuits chose as their motto *Ad Majorem Dei*

Gloriam, a Latin phrase that means "for the greater glory of God." This would be the standard for all their missions.

Ironically, as his young Jesuits embarked on various apostolic adventures around the world, the fifty-year-old Ignatius stayed put. Until his death in 1556, he managed the Society from his desk in Rome, sending others to labor all over the world while penning thousands of letters of instruction and encouragement. As superior general, Ignatius had great love for his fellow Jesuits, but he did not hesitate to challenge them. During these years in Rome, he also wrote the constitutions of his fledgling order, fine-tuned the *Spiritual Exercises*, and continued to give the retreat to people from all walks of life.

Ignatius died on July 31, 1556, after suffering the effects of a persistent stomach ailment. At his death, the Society numbered nearly one thousand men, with houses and colleges stretching from Brazil to across Europe and Japan. Ignatius was canonized, together with Francis Xavier, in 1622.

Over the years, the young knight's desire for power, prestige, and privilege had been transformed—by God's grace—into a desire for a life of prayer, service, and simplicity. Gradually, Ignatius grew in his awareness of God's deep love not just for the world generally but for himself personally. He experienced this love as a profoundly intimate call by Christ to follow him, a call that filled Ignatius with a passionate zeal to serve God and to help souls.

For Ignatius and the Society of Jesus, the primary instrument to discern God's call in our lives is the Spiritual Exercises. Through the Exercises, we grow in faith, hope, and love. In them, we prepare for and sustain ourselves in the service of God and others. More than a book, the Exercises are an experience, a great adventure to the heart of God and, therefore, to the real and present needs of the world.

The Ignatian Adventure

As we've seen, Ignatius of Loyola as a young man left his family home in Spain to embark on an adventure that would transform countless lives, beginning with his own. Traveling across Europe and the Mediterranean, he would learn that the greatest adventures in life were not always geographic. The adventure that God had in store for Ignatius was about traveling the distance between the head and the heart and about inspiring in Ignatius bold, holy desires for God's greater glory and the service of others.

Ignatius gave the church the Spiritual Exercises as a testament to God's gentle, persistent laboring in his life. Over his lifetime, Ignatius became convinced that the Exercises could help other people draw closer to God and discern God's call in their lives, much as they had helped him.

The Exercises have never been for Jesuits alone. Ignatius crafted the Exercises as a layman, and he intended them to benefit the entire church. He honed them as he offered the Exercises to a variety of people. Inspired by the Second Vatican Council, the Society of Jesus has continued to offer the Exercises in varied and creative ways to ever-increasing numbers of people.

By making the Spiritual Exercises available and leading people through them, Jesuits share their heritage with the world, including with their students and colleagues in ministry. This is especially important as laypersons assume more active roles in Jesuit universities, schools, parishes, and other works. This book offers one way that the Exercises may be offered to individuals and groups. Before exploring the different ways that this book can be used, let's look more carefully at the time-tested genius of the Exercises.

Spiritual Exercises

People interested in the Exercises may be familiar with other spiritual classics, such as those by John of the Cross, Teresa of Ávila, Thomas Merton, or Dorothy Day. Such books can be read privately and prayerfully. Their style may be mystical, poetic, or descriptive. The books have the form of narrative or exhortation. The *Spiritual Exercises* is nothing like those works. Ignatius's *Exercises* makes for very dry reading—it's more like reading a cookbook or how-to guide. The retreatant need not even read the book of the *Exercises* because Ignatius intended the book as a manual for spiritual directors or guides to lead others through the Exercises (*SE* 2). In one sense, there is nothing new in the Exercises: Ignatius relied on prayer forms and spiritual traditions deeply rooted in the church. What is distinctive is how Ignatius artfully weaves them together and how much he emphasizes the experiential and practical in the life of prayer.

Thus, the **purpose of the Exercises** is very practical: to grow in union with God, who frees us to make good decisions about our lives and to "help souls." Ignatius invites us into an intimate encounter with God, revealed in Jesus Christ, so that we can learn to think and act more like Christ. The Exercises help us grow in interior freedom from sin and disordered loves so that we can respond more generously to God's call in our life (*SE* 2, 21). The Exercises demand much of us, engaging our intellect and emotions, our memory and will. Making the Exercises can be both exhilarating and exhausting; it's no wonder that Ignatius compared making the Spiritual Exercises to doing physical exercise, such as "taking a walk, traveling on foot, and running" (*SE* 1).

The Exercises are a school of prayer. The two primary forms of praying taught in the Exercises are meditation and contemplation.

In **meditation**, we use our intellect to wrestle with basic principles that guide our life. Reading Scripture, we pray over words, images, and ideas. We engage our memory to appreciate the activity of God in our life. Such insights into who God is and who we are before God allow our hearts to be moved.

Contemplation is more about feeling than thinking. Contemplation often stirs the emotions and inspires deep, God-given desires. In contemplation, we rely on our imaginations to place ourselves in a setting from the Gospels or in a scene proposed by Ignatius. Scripture has a central place in the Exercises because it is the revelation of who God is, particularly in Jesus Christ, and of what God does in our world. *In the Exercises, we pray with Scripture; we do not study it.* Although Scripture study is central to any believer's faith, we leave for another time extended biblical exegesis and theological investigation.

The Movements of the Exercises

The Exercises have a natural rhythm. Ignatius divides the Exercises into four "weeks" (*SE* 4). These weeks are not calendar weeks but phases or movements felt within a person who is praying through the Exercises:

- **Preparation Days:** Just as marathon runners do not begin a race with a sprint, we start the Exercises slowly and gently. We till the soil a bit before doing any planting. In the first days of the full Exercises, we consider the gift of God's ongoing creation in the world and in us. We pray for a spirit of awe and gratitude for the gifts of God in our lives. We hope to experience a deeply felt sense of God's unconditional love for us.

- **First Week:** Having recognized God's boundless generosity to us, we naturally face our own limited response. We let God reveal to us our sinfulness and need for conversion. We acknowledge how we have misused God's gift of freedom.

With God's help, we recognize and understand the patterns of sin in our lives. We do so in the context of knowing deep down how much God loves us and wants to free us from everything that gets in the way of loving God, others, and ourselves—that is, from everything that makes us unhappy. We pray for the grace of embracing ourselves as loved sinners. We keep our gaze fixed always on God's mercy.

- **Second Week:** Having experienced God's faithful love, we are moved to respond with greater generosity. We want to love and serve God and others more. As we pray through the life of Jesus Christ presented in the Gospels, we ask to know him more intimately so that we can love him more dearly and follow him more closely. We come to appreciate Jesus' values and his vision of the world. This heartfelt knowing that leads to concrete action is a defining grace of the Exercises.

- **Third Week:** Our deepening personal identification with Jesus inspires us to want to be with him in his suffering and death. We spend time contemplating the Lord's passion, which is the consummate expression of God's faithfulness and love for us.

- **Fourth Week:** Just as we accompany Jesus in the Passion, we walk with the Risen Lord in the joy of the resurrected life. We continue to learn from him as he consoles others. Having savored God's love for us and our world, we pray with a generous heart to find God in all things, to love and serve God and others in concrete ways and with great enthusiasm.

A caution: neatly laying out the retreat in this way can be misleading, as though we were in control. To the contrary, we follow the lead of the Spirit, as Ignatius did, and the Spirit may lead us through some twists and turns along the way. We should not follow the book of the Exercises in a mechanical way because God works with each of us so uniquely. A trusted mentor or spiritual guide can help us navigate these movements of the soul.

Discernment

The **discernment of spirits** underlies the expanse of the Exercises. The one who discerns is like the adventurers who test the winds or check a compass to make sure they're heading in the right direction. In discernment of spirits, we notice the interior movements of our hearts, which include our thoughts, feelings, desires, attractions, and resistances. We determine where they are coming from and where they are leading us; and then we propose to act in a way that leads to greater faith, hope, and love. A regular practice of discernment helps us make good decisions.

In the course of the Exercises, some people make important life decisions. The decision may concern a significant relationship, a career or religious vocation, or a change in lifestyle or habits of living. The Exercises provide many helps in making such decisions. The key is being open to the Spirit, who will present us with these decisions and guide us in making them. For others, the Exercises are not about making a big decision about what to do but about how to be. In other words, they teach us how to live, think, pray, love, and relate in the context of commitments we've already made.

As with any genuine adventure, we cannot know at the outset where we will end up. But we can be assured that God, who is always faithful, will be with us and will lead us where we need to go. Though uncertain of where our journey will end, we know where it begins: here and now. God chose to become one of us in Jesus Christ, living in the beauty and brokenness of our world. It is in *this* place and *this* time, in the details of our individual lives, where we meet God.

By even exploring an invitation to make the Exercises in some form, you have taken the first step on the journey and revealed a generous spirit. Ignatius commends such magnanimity at the opening of the Exercises:

> The persons who make the Exercises will benefit greatly by entering upon them with great spirit and generosity toward their Creator and Lord, and by offering all their desires and freedom to him so that His Divine Majesty can make use of their persons and of all they possess in whatsoever way is in accord with his most holy will. (*SE* 5)

Such courage, openness, and generosity are attributes of adventurers following in the footsteps of Ignatius. He has blazed for us a fascinating trail, which runs from his life to Christ's life through our very own. To better understand where our particular trail begins, we now explore the different ways we may experience the Exercises and make use of this particular guidebook.

Different Paths, Same Journey

THE BOOK OF THE *SPIRITUAL EXERCISES* opens with twenty preliminary notes, or annotations. A theme runs through these notes: **adaptability**. Ignatius's own conversion taught him that God works with each person uniquely, so he insisted that the Exercises be adapted to meet the particular needs of the one making them. The goal is drawing closer to God, not mechanically running through all of the exercises in order or in unison with others. In other words, the end of the Exercises is a Person, not a performance.

Ways of Making the Exercises

Some people have the opportunity to make the Exercises over thirty or more consecutive days, usually removed from regular life in a retreat house setting. This retreat is described in the **twentieth annotation**. (Jesuits make this "long retreat" at least twice in their lives.) Ignatius realized that many people do not have the luxury of time or resources to make a thirty-day retreat. Thus, in the **nineteenth annotation**, he describes how a person may be directed through the entirety of the Exercises but over an extended period of time, while continuing his or her ordinary daily affairs. Others, because of age, experience, life circumstance, or time constraints, cannot cover the full breadth of the Exercises. Instead, they pray through particular parts of the Exercises, such as during a weekend or weeklong retreat or a day of prayer. This is an **eighteenth-annotation** retreat.

The preliminary notes reveal Ignatius's intention to offer the Exercises to many people, but in different ways. We should resist judging one way of making the Exercises against another, as if one way were superior. Instead, the adaptability of the Exercises poses the question, Which way is most suitable to the person desiring to make the Exercises?

How This Book Can Be Used

Even within each format for making the Exercises there is ample room for adaptation. This book offers such flexibility and can be used by those who are creatively adapting the Exercises to meet the needs of people today. However it is used, this book, like the text of the Spiritual Exercises itself, is to be experienced, not read. It's a handy guide that invites pray-ers to encounter the living God, who is active in their lives and the larger world.

First, the book may be used in its entirety to facilitate an eight-month-long retreat in daily life. In the pages that follow, there are thirty-two weeks of prayer, with suggestions for every day. For a nineteenth-annotation retreat like this, the more traditional practice is for the retreatant to pray daily on his or her own and then meet one-on-one with a spiritual director every week or so. The spiritual director, who serves as a guide for the journey, is central to the Exercises offered in this format. The director listens to the experience of retreatants and helps them discern the movement of God in their prayer and in daily events. The director may adapt the outline of the retreat presented in this book to the particular circumstances of a retreatant.

As important as the role of the director is, Ignatius reminds us in the introductory notes to the Exercises that the chief spiritual director is God, who communicates with each person. The director should make every effort not to get in the way:

It is more appropriate and far better that the Creator and Lord himself should communicate himself to the devout soul, embracing it in love and praise, and disposing it for the way which will enable the soul to serve him better in the future. Accordingly, the one giving the Exercises ought not to lean or incline in either direction but rather, while standing by like the pointer on a scale in equilibrium, to allow the Creator to deal immediately with the creature and the creature with its Creator and Lord. (*SE* 15)

In recent years, Jesuit universities, high schools, and parishes have experimented with this traditional model because there was a great demand for the Exercises but not enough directors to meet with each retreatant individually. One adaptation that has proved successful is to offer the Exercises to groups of pray-ers. Instead of meeting one-on-one with a director, retreatants meet in a small group facilitated by a director. Even if a person makes the Exercises individually with a director, he or she may enjoy getting together with others who are making the Exercises. Some Jesuit institutions offer monthly gatherings for those on retreat in daily life to share the graces of the retreat and to listen to presentations about the Exercises. Such gatherings help to build community and to bolster the Ignatian identity of a university, school, or parish.

Second, the book may be used to help structure shorter experiences of prayer. A person or group might pray the Exercises in discrete blocks. The book is divided into five segments based on Ignatius's "weeks," which may be helpful in arranging such prayer experiences. One creative approach may be to adapt the prayer materials to the liturgical season—for example, praying with the Third Week material during Lent or with the Fourth Week material during the Easter season.

Third, for those who have made the Exercises before, the book may serve as a helpful way to deepen some of those graces. Such an experienced pray-er may skip around to different parts of the book to revisit the Exercises, all depending on where God is leading him or her.

Finally, for someone who is looking for structure in personal prayer life, the book may be a helpful companion because it offers suggestions for prayer around various themes. Such pray-ers shouldn't try to make the Exercises from start to finish on their own, without the help of an experienced guide. But certainly they can use the book to dip their toes in the water, to become familiar with the rhythm and techniques of Ignatian prayer. The rules for discernment of spirits scattered throughout the book may also be helpful for people seeking to ground decisions and values in their faith.

Although the Exercises are a valuable gift to God's people, they are not for everyone. Ignatius would be the first to insist that the Exercises are only a means to an end. There are other ways of praying that help us grow in intimacy with God and that inspire a life of service to others. But if a person is called to experience the Spiritual Exercises in some form, he or she is in for an exciting, unpredictable, challenging, and perhaps life-changing adventure.

Preparing for the Adventure

Before beginning the Spiritual Exercises, you must carefully discern whether you're ready for the adventure and in what way you will travel. The Exercises in the format of the nineteenth annotation (the full Exercises) require a significant commitment of time and energy. They presuppose that retreatants are already in a habit of praying and are comfortable talking about their interior life and their faith with a spiritual director or group. *No one should feel any less about themselves simply because they choose not to begin or continue with the Exercises in this form.*

Some may choose instead to experience Ignatian prayer in a shorter format or to commit themselves to praying more regularly but without excessive structure, using some of the techniques in this book.

For those beginning to pray with the Exercises in some form, Ignatius offers some helpful advice to prepare for the adventure. We are wise to follow his counsel. His suggestions will help you develop a rhythm and pace of prayer, which you can adjust and personalize as you progress in whatever retreat form you've chosen.

First, commit to spending **thirty to forty-five minutes per day** in private, personal prayer. You need an extended period of time to engage the prayer material deeply and savor the graces offered. If you are not in the habit of praying that long in one sitting, then slowly build up to that time in the weeks leading up to the retreat. To help you establish a habit of praying, try praying at the same time each day.

Find a regular **prayer space**: a quiet room in your home with a comfortable chair, a favorite church or chapel, even a secluded place outside. It is often helpful to keep the same prayer space throughout the retreat: such regularity helps you ease into prayer. To remind you that this space is sacred, mark it with a candle, icon, painting, photograph, rosary, or crucifix. If it's helpful and not distracting, light incense or play soft, meditative music.

This book suggests material to pray over: Scripture passages, Ignatius's meditations and contemplations, or other exercises. Look over these materials before you formally begin your prayer period—either the evening or morning before (*SE* 73–74). This preparation allows you to sort through any questions or confusion about the prayer material itself, thus removing unnecessary mental clutter from your prayer period. You can dive right in when you go to your prayer space.

In the time immediately before your prayer period, avoid sensory or information overload. Turn off the television, radio, and iPod; don't check e-mail or browse the Internet; turn off your cell phone. This discipline will make transitioning into the quiet of prayer easier.

Because you are praying the Exercises in the midst of your daily life, it is important to tell others with whom you live about the retreat. You will likely need the support of family and close friends during the retreat. They can help you very practically by giving you the time and space to pray each day.

In addition to structuring your day and your environment, you will benefit by ordering, at least at first, your time of prayer (or "prayer period"):

Compose Yourself

Ignatius writes:

> A step or two away from the place where I will make my contemplation or meditation, I will stand for the length of an Our Father. I will raise my mind and think how God our Lord is looking

at me, and other such thoughts. Then I will make
an act of reverence or humility. (*SE* 75)

- Imagine how God looks upon you: with great joy and gratitude for your offering of time. Imagine God's long, loving
  gaze upon you.

- Once you are in your prayer space, still yourself. Although it is
  sometimes hard to settle your mind, you can relax your body
  by breathing deeply and slowly. With each breath, you may
  utter a short mantra, such as "God be with me," "My Lord
  and my God," "Come, Holy Spirit," or something similar.

- In prayer, the body and spirit work together. Find a posture
  conducive to prayer: sit, kneel, stand, or recline in a relaxed
  position (*SE* 76). Finding a comfortable posture will keep
  you from changing it as you pray, which can be distracting.
  Also, beware that you are not so relaxed that you fall asleep!

- Ask God to be with you in this time of prayer. In words that
  flow naturally, make a simple offering of your time, attention, and energies. For example, Ignatius suggests one such
  preparatory prayer:

  > Ask God our Lord for the grace that all my
  > intentions, actions, and operations may be
  > ordered purely to the service and praise of the
  > Divine Majesty. (*SE* 46)

- In making the offering, you remind yourself at the outset
  that you are not thinking about God but encountering God
  in a very real way.

Pray for the Grace

Recall from Ignatius's conversion story how God gently but
steadily transformed his zeal and passion from serving the king

and winning the love of a lady to serving the church for the greater glory of God. Ignatian spirituality taps into our deepest desires. In them we can discern God's noble desires for us.

Thus, at the beginning of each prayer period, Ignatius advises that we pray for a certain grace, or gift from God: "ask God our Lord for what I want and desire" (*SE* 48). Simply naming what we deeply desire opens us to receive the gift God wants to give us. Moreover, praying for a grace helps us to notice when we actually receive that gift later on. In this way, we realize that the grace is not of our own making but is the result of God's generosity to us. Finally, praying out of our desires grounds us in the present, keeping our prayer "real."

Throughout the retreat, Ignatius suggests specific graces to pray for. Always feel free to articulate a different grace or to use different words if the Spirit is moving you in that direction. Imagine God asking you, "What do you want me to do for you?"

Some graces are hard to ask for. For example, in all honesty, you may resist asking to let go of a preoccupation or way of thinking or acting that is comfortable for you. Or you may hesitate in asking to be placed with Christ, carrying the cross. Such resistance is understandable. If you find yourself resisting a suggested grace, then pray not for the grace itself but for a desire to want the grace. For example, "Lord, I'm really having a hard time asking to walk with you by living a more simple life; for now, give me the desire to want to do that."

Although grace is revealed in the particular gifts God gives you, grace above all is God's presence in your life. The Giver is the gift!

Do the Prayer

Having taken some time to compose yourself and center your mind and heart, engage the material presented in the book or suggested by your spiritual director. This book provides exercises for every day of the calendar week, but do not feel that you need to go through the days mechanically. The goal is God, not the book! Don't worry about missing something if you skip around. God will give you what you need.

Ignatius leaves room to adapt the Exercises to meet you where you are, emotionally and spiritually, during the retreat. This **flexibility** is especially important during a retreat in everyday life, when some person, problem, or experience may become the focus of your prayer or when you spend several prayer periods lingering over one meditation or contemplation.

Close Your Prayer

Just as you begin your prayer time with certain rituals or prayers, you should formally bring your prayer to a close. You can conclude with a favorite prayer, such as the Our Father or Hail Mary, or with another prayer of your choosing. You might spontaneously pray to God the Father, to Jesus, or to Mary in a very conversational manner. Use your body to mark the closing of prayer: such as with a bow, by making the sign of the cross, or with an open gesture of the hands or arms (*SE* 75).

Review the Prayer

Ignatius advises that *after* we formally close our prayer, we reflect on our experience of prayer (*SE* 77). Keeping a journal is most helpful during a retreat. This exercise can be challenging because we are trying to put into words our encounter with God, who is Holy Mystery. Although it is challenging, trying to articulate such sublime experiences can help us discern how God is meeting us or leading us in our prayer. As a practical matter, journaling helps us prepare for meetings with a spiritual director or retreat group. The journal is for your eyes only. When the retreat concludes, the journal becomes a rich spiritual treasure to which you can return months or even years after the retreat.

The purpose of journaling is not to replay your time of prayer minute by minute. Instead, after your prayer period concludes, consider the following:

- What were the significant interior movements (that is, feelings, reactions, intuitions, desires, emotions, thoughts, or insights)?

- What was the prevailing mood of my prayer: peace, agitation, excitement, boredom, confusion, calm?

- Was my prayer more about the head or the heart, or about both?

- What word, phrase, image, or memory meant most to me during prayer?

- Is there some unfinished business that I think God is calling me to return to during another time of prayer?

- Is there something happening in my life that is becoming part of my prayer? Do I feel moved to do something concrete in my life?

- Am I making the necessary preparations for my prayer? Is there anything I am doing or not doing that is getting in the way of my listening to God?

The review of prayer is not homework; do not feel bound to answer each of these questions every time you journal. Instead, consider journaling as another way of praying, of going deeper to sift through the graces. Write in a style that is comfortable for you. In your journaling, feel free to write directly to God the Father or to Jesus, as if you were writing a letter or an e-mail.

These guidelines reflect the wisdom of St. Ignatius and retreat directors who are committed to Ignatian ways of praying. However helpful they may be, the guidelines are not a magic formula that will automatically summon certain graces. We cannot control the movement of God in our lives, but we can take concrete steps to make ourselves more open and receptive to how God speaks to us.

A Note to Spiritual Directors and Retreat Leaders

IN THE FOLLOWING PAGES, I outline thirty-two weeks of a nineteenth-annotation retreat, with prayer material for each of the seven days in a week. Keeping in mind Ignatius's insistence on adaptability, adjust the retreat to meet the needs of your retreatants or to accommodate the schedule at your university, school, or parish. The book can be taken in parts, adapting the retreat into shorter periods based on a theme or liturgical season. The prayer material is ample, which allows you to extend or condense days or weeks as you see fit.

With this book in hand, some retreatants may put pressure on themselves to "get through" the book. Or if you stay with some prayer material longer than others, they may think that they are doing something wrong or not keeping up with others. Point out these reactions for what they are: needless pressures and distractions.

Some retreatants, particularly those prone to perfectionism, may worry that they will miss something if they do not follow all the days as planned. Assure them that with God as our ultimate spiritual director, it is unlikely that we'll miss something important! You can also offer the following image if it's helpful: praying through the Exercises is more like moving along a spiral than making a linear progression; we keep returning to key graces, considering them in different ways, deepening them as we go along.

We gaze upon Jesus from different vantage points, getting to know him more and more intimately.

After the sixth week of prayer material, I suggest discerning with retreatants whether to continue with the Exercises. Such discernment is critical before moving to considerations of sin and God's mercy in Ignatius's **First Week**. Some may find that the preparatory material has been enough to jump-start their prayer life. Others may struggle in finding the time and energy to pray formally through the Exercises. Remember, the Exercises are not an end in themselves—they are only one means of building a more intimate relationship with God and putting faith into action. It is not a failure to end a retreat after careful discernment. The retreatant simply learns to shift gears and pray in a different way.

I offer my own version of the Examen at the end of the preparatory weeks, but you may decide to introduce this prayer at another time. Honoring the priority that Ignatius placed on the Examen as a way of praying, we should encourage retreatants to integrate the Examen into their daily practice of prayer early in the retreat.

As spiritual guides, we walk with retreatants through the Exercises. We pray that our faithfulness and attentiveness to them mirrors God's surpassing care. Although we keep our focus on the retreatants' experience of God, we realize that the adventure is not for them alone. In the Exercises, directors, too, meet the living God. We thus begin the adventure with great gratitude, humility, and expectation.

The Adventure Begins

✝

Encountering the Unconditional, Creative,
Inviting Love of God

My ADVENTURE IN THE JESUITS began in Syracuse, New York, where I entered the novitiate for the Maryland and New York provinces. The novitiate is the first two years of a Jesuit's formation, during which Ignatius prescribed certain "experiments" to test the man's vocation and to hone his noble desires to serve God and help others. One of these experiences is the thirty-day version of the Spiritual Exercises, which Jesuit novices (those who have not yet taken vows) make during their first year in the novitiate. Another is an experience of working with the sick, one of the corporal works of mercy.

Six of us were sent to a palliative care center in the Bronx for our hospital "experiment." We were not sent as chaplains. Instead, we were assigned to do the work of an orderly or caregiver: feeding, bathing, dressing, and otherwise caring for the physical needs of the patients. The patients in Calvary Hospital in the Catholic Archdiocese of New York were mostly at the end stages of cancer, AIDS, or other terminal illnesses. They came to Calvary not to be cured but to be made comfortable and to find peace with their dying.

Calvary is a special place, not simply because of its distinctive mission to care for the whole person—mind, body, and spirit—but also because of the patients and their families who come there. Many years later, I can still see their faces and recall their stories.

Leonard suffered from leukemia. He and his wife, Elaine, were in their seventies or eighties, both gentle souls. On most days, Elaine kept a silent vigil by her husband's bed, watching him slip gradually into unconsciousness. One day I offered to feed and wash Leonard to give the tired Elaine a break. I noticed purplish marks on his forearm, which were faded and matched the color of his veins, readily apparent through his aging skin. Washing Leonard's hands, I realized that the marks were numbers, an indelible reminder of his time in a concentration camp in Eastern Europe. Elaine noticed that I saw the numbers. We exchanged no words, only a knowing glance. As I continued to go about my care, I imagined the life Leonard had lived in the fifty or so years since his first encounter with death. The contrast between the clean, peaceful, nurturing setting he lay in and the one he faced in a concentration camp—where many did not leave—was jarring.

There was a quiet dignity in the work at Calvary. All were welcome, regardless of religious tradition or socioeconomic background. The physicians and nursing staff chose to work there, knowing that most of their patients would die in their care. But they die with dignity, with care for their body and soul, in the company of their families. For the homeless brought there, the hospital staff become their family.

I came to Calvary uncomfortable with hospitals and very nervous about having to feed and wash strangers (we bathed and changed only the male patients). Fortunately, we novices were assigned nurses or caregivers who served as our mentors. When I met Rhona, all my self-concerns slipped away, thanks to her warm, inviting smile and her calm assurances uttered in a soothing Caribbean accent: "Everything will be fine, brother. Just watch and follow what I do." She had trained other young Jesuits in the past, so she knew what kind of reluctance and discomfort I was experiencing.

Rhona taught me the basics: how to get patients to eat when they did not want to; how to change a bed when a patient was still in it (a feat I'm still proud of to this day); how to change a patient's diaper in the most efficient and respectful way; how to deal with the variety of emotions that a family brought to the hospital; how to clean out a patient's mouth; and how to give an enema. I barely got through that last learning experience. I can still hear her voice: "Keep looking at his face, brother. Look at the relief that you are giving him."

Rhona taught me much about the logistics of a patient's care. More important, she showed me how much physical care and spiritual care are intertwined. She, as much as my Jesuit mentors, schooled me in how to minister to people. Whether patients were conscious or not, Rhona would always talk to them ("You never know what they can hear" was her refrain.) She never talked down to them. She asked their permission to change or bathe them. She stroked their hair to tell them how beautiful they looked. She was able to diffuse uneasy situations with a ready laugh. Rhona never pretended that the patients were not dying. In her graceful presence, she honored where each patient and his or her family existed on the continuum of life and death. She helped patients die with dignity and, in her own way, eased the transition from this world to their life with God in heaven.

Rhona watched many people die over her years of service. Mr. Jackson was one of our favorite patients. We were both in the room when he died. He didn't speak, but he groaned, hummed, smiled, and grimaced to tell us exactly how we were doing. His daughter came to visit after work, so we were alone with him most days. Mr. Jackson never put up much fuss when I needed to bathe or change him. There was something innately kind about this man. As I cared for him each day, I wondered what Mr. Jackson's story was: where he was from, what he did for a living, whom he had married. If we die the way we live, then Mr. Jackson led a most gracious life.

We knew patients were dying when their breathing became very labored and when their bodies rejected nourishment. Mr. Jackson's body started to shut down. His daughter was there as he neared death, but it was Rhona who held his hand and brushed his forehead. I can hear her now: "It's OK, Mr. Jackson. You can let go. Your daughter is here, you are surrounded by love. Now go on. Go on and meet the Lord. He's waiting for you. Your wife is waiting for you. Everything is going to be all right." His eyes opened, a bit glazed over. But he looked toward Rhona, and I know he saw her smile, one of this world's last gifts to him.

A fundamental truth underlies the Exercises: that God, the Creator of all, loves us unconditionally, and we, in our beauty and even our limitation, enjoy a special worth and dignity in the eyes of God. Our Creator reminds us of this divine embrace by lavishing on us so many gifts: in nature, in our own talents, in the people around us, in the gifts of the earth. The most natural response to this gracious love and God's faithfulness is to love God in return, to reverence the gifts of God, and to love others as we have been loved so unconditionally.

In the first days of the Exercises, Ignatius invites us to pray through these basic truths as revealed in Scripture, in nature, and in our own inspired memory. These truths are so deep that they take a lifetime to appreciate fully; with a love as deep as God's, it's no wonder we never really figure it out. But we do live these truths. We see them in action, as I did at Calvary hospital—each patient a child of God, each person treated with dignity, each one with a sacred story. Rhona and her colleagues there, who work year in and year out, as Jesuit novices come and go—they are tangible reminders of God's unconditional and faithful love, lived out in daily feedings, gentle baths, clean sheets, and words of reassurance at the end of life.

A Prayer by Thomas Merton

My Lord God, I have no idea where I am going.
I do not see the road ahead of me.
I cannot know for certain where it will end.
Nor do I really know myself,
and the fact that I think I am following your will
does not mean that I am actually doing so.

But I believe that the desire to please you does in fact please you.
And I hope I have that desire in all that I am doing.
I hope that I will never do anything apart from that desire.
And I know that if I do this you will lead me by the right road,
though I may know nothing about it.

Therefore will I trust you always
though I may seem to be lost and in the shadow of death.
I will not fear, for you are ever with me,
and you will never leave me to face my perils alone.

THOMAS MERTON (1915–1968) is one of the most prolific spiritual writers of the past century. A convert to Catholicism, he entered the Trappist monastery of Gethsemane outside Louisville, Kentucky, in 1941. The author of more than sixty books and hundreds of articles and poems, Merton's most acclaimed book is his spiritual autobiography, *The Seven Storey Mountain*.

Week of Prayer #1:
God's Unconditional Love for Me

We begin the retreat by reflecting on God's faithful, unconditional love for each of us. We consider who we are most fundamentally—or rather, *Whose* we are. Each one of us is God's beloved son or daughter: this is the core of our identity.

I suggest prayer points for each day of the week. These are only suggestions; remember that adaptability is a hallmark of the Spiritual Exercises. Do not feel that you must run through the Scripture passages as if you were completing homework. You may choose to stay with one or two passages all week. Follow the lead of the Spirit and the counsel of your spiritual guide if you have one.

At the beginning of each prayer period, we pray for a certain grace: *What do I desire? What do I want during this time of prayer?* For Ignatius, tapping into our desires was a way to keep prayer grounded in reality. Moreover, naming what we want also helps us open up to receive the expected and unexpected gifts of God.

Each week, I suggest a certain grace, but do not be bound by my wording or the specific grace I propose. Let your praying for the grace flow from the heart above all else.

† Prayer for the Week

I pray for the following graces: to be more aware of how God is near; to trust in God's personal care and love for me.

DAY 1

Read Isaiah 43:1–7 ("I have called you by name, you are mine"). Pray slowly over the verses. What words or images move you? Consider: *Who is God for me? How does God see me?*

DAY 2

Read Luke 12:22–34 (Do not worry; God cares for me as for the lilies of the field). Consider: *What worries or fears do I want to let go of as I begin the retreat?*

DAY 3

Read Psalm 23 ("The LORD is my shepherd"). Pray slowly and quietly over these verses; say them out loud as you would a poem. Consider: *What words or images move me?*

DAY 4

Read Psalm 131 ("I have calmed and quieted my soul, like a weaned child with its mother"). Practice resting in the Lord; be still and quiet, not busying your prayer. Consider: *What words or images spring from my heart or imagination?*

DAY 5

Read Psalm 139:1–18 ("O LORD, you have searched me and known me"). Consider: *How does God gaze upon me? How open am I to receiving this intimacy?*

DAY 6

Read Isaiah 43:1–7 or Psalm 139:1–18. Pray through one of these Scriptures again. Note in your journal the gifts and talents God has given you. Note, too, your very human limitations or weaknesses. Remember that God loves us as we are.

DAY 7

Savor the graces of the week. Prayerfully review your journal. Remember the key graces and give thanks to God for them.

Talk about your week with God the Father, with Jesus, or with Mary. Return to any words, Scripture passages, images, or memories that meant a lot to you.

For Further Reflection

As we enter into the Spiritual Exercises which follow, we retreatants find ourselves sometimes doing much thinking and reasoning things out. At other times, we experience far more the response of our hearts, with little or nothing for the head to be concerned about. It is good to remember that we are always in the context of prayer, whether the prayer is more meditative or more affective. We should always try to maintain a spirit of deep reverence before God, especially when our affections are involved.

Anima Christi (traditional translation)

Soul of Christ, sanctify me.
Body of Christ, save me.
Blood of Christ, inebriate me.
Water from the side of Christ, wash me.
Passion of Christ, strengthen me.
O good Jesus, hear me.
Within your wounds hide me.
Do not allow me to be separated from you.
From the malevolent enemy defend me.
In the hour of my death call me,
and bid me come to you,
that with your saints I may praise you
forever and ever. Amen.

The *Anima Christi* ("Soul of Christ") was a popular prayer in Ignatius's day. Ignatius does not include the prayer in the original text of his Exercises, but he does refer to it several times. Many later editions of the Exercises include this prayer at the beginning. It serves to remind us that Jesus Christ is central to the Exercises.

Anima Christi (contemporary translation)

Jesus, may all that is you flow into me.
May your body and blood be my food and drink.
May your passion and death be my strength and life.
Jesus, with you by my side, enough has been given.
May the shelter I seek be the shadow of your cross.
Let me not run from the love which you offer,
But hold me safe from the forces of evil.
On each of my dyings shed your light and your love.
Keep calling to me until that day comes, when, with your saints,
I may praise you forever. Amen.

This is David Fleming's paraphrase of the third annotation from the Spiritual Exercises, in *Draw Me into Your Friendship: The Spiritual Exercises—A Literal Translation and a Contemporary Reading.*

The "Presupposition" of the Spiritual Exercises

THE RELATIONSHIP BETWEEN THE SPIRITUAL director and the retreatant is central to the Exercises. To facilitate effective communication and build an atmosphere of trust, Ignatius suggests some guiding principles as the retreat opens. He groups this advice under the heading, "Presupposition."

> That both the giver and the maker of the Spiritual Exercises may be of greater help and benefit to each other, it should be presupposed that every good Christian ought to be more eager to put a good interpretation on a neighbor's statement than to condemn it.
>
> Further, if one cannot interpret it favorably, one should ask how the other means it. If that meaning is wrong, one should correct the person with love; and if this is not enough, one should search out every appropriate means through which, by understanding the statement in a good way, it may be saved. (*SE* 22)

The Presupposition is often called the Ignatian "plus sign." As much as possible, put a positive interpretation on another's statement. Resolve confusion and misinterpretation up front. Correct another's error in a spirit of humility and charity.

These very practical suggestions apply not only to spiritual direction relationships but also to any human interaction. The Presupposition also facilitates conversation in groups making the Exercises.

Week of Prayer #2:
God's Ongoing Creation

GOD CREATES NOT JUST AT one point in time, but continually. God's creative, life-giving Spirit animates us and all of creation. During his convalescence at Loyola, Ignatius encountered God in nature. In his autobiography, dictated in the third person, he writes of himself: "The greatest consolation he received at this time was from gazing at the sky and stars, and this he often did and for quite a long time" (*Autobiography*, no. 11).

This week, we pray with our ancestors in faith as they marvel at the goodness and ongoing activity of God in creation. You may choose to make one or more of your prayer periods outside, soaking in the natural beauty of creation. Use all of your senses to experience the world. This week, as you walk the streets and go about your daily tasks, be attentive to the variety of God's creations, especially in the people you encounter.

Many of the psalms we find in Scripture were originally hymns sung at Jewish festivals and worship services. They read like poetry. Thus, try reading the psalms out loud when you pray. You may also want to write a psalm of your own in your journal.

† Prayer for the Week

I pray for the following graces: wonder at God's ongoing creation; gratitude for the gift of God creating me and creating the world.

Day 1

Read Psalm 8. Marvel at the dignity of the human person. Give thanks to God for particular people who reveal God's loving presence to you. Consider: *Who has helped me get to this point in my faith journey?*

Day 2

Read Psalm 104. God is revealed in the natural world. All is a gift to us. With the psalmist, give thanks for the glory of God's creation. Consider: *Where do I see this awesome glory revealed in my life and the larger world?*

Day 3

Read Genesis 1:26–2:9. Consider these two accounts of the creation of humanity. Listen to God declare creation "very good." Consider yourself as God's creation, as an incarnation, or image of God in a particular time, family, and place. Rejoice in the fact of your existence as God's creation, even amid the complexities of human life.

Day 4

Read Romans 8:18–25 (All creation is unfinished and yearns for fulfillment in God). Consider: *What are the particular high-lights or milestones of my life, including my life of faith?* Note both the highs and the lows, the times of great hope and of challenge or "groaning."

Day 5

Read Psalm 33 ("Our soul waits for the LORD. . . . Our heart is glad in him"). Consider: *What am I waiting for? How is my heart filled with gladness?*

Day 6

Read Jeremiah 18:1–6 (We are like clay in the potter's hands). Consider: *How do I find myself being shaped and molded by God now? How am I pliable or resistant?*

Day 7

Read prayerfully Mary Oliver's poem "Messenger." She reminds us that our basic work in life is "learning to be astonished" at the beauty around us and in us. Practice being astonished.

Messenger

My work is loving the world.
Here the sunflowers, there the hummingbird—
    equal seekers of sweetness.
Here the quickening yeast; there the blue plums.
Here the clam deep in the speckled sand.

Are my boots old? Is my coat torn?
Am I no longer young, and still not half-perfect? Let me
    keep my mind on what matters,
which is my work,

which is mostly standing still and learning to be
    astonished.
The phoebe, the delphinium.
The sheep in the pasture, and the pasture.
Which is mostly rejoicing, since all the ingredients are here,

which is gratitude, to be given a mind and a heart
    and these body-clothes,
a mouth with which to give shouts of joy
    to the moth and the wren, to the sleepy dug-up clam,
telling them all, over and over, how it is
    that we live forever.

—MARY OLIVER, *THIRST: POEMS BY MARY OLIVER*

For Further Reflection

Prayer, understood as the distilled awareness of our entire life before God, is a journey forward, a response to a call from the Father to become perfectly like his Son through the power of the Holy Spirit. But this journey forward can also be seen as a kind of journey backward, in which we seek to gain access to the relationship Adam had with God.

In prayer we journey forward to our origin. We close our eyes in prayer and open them in the pristine moment of creation. We open our eyes to find God, his hands still smeared with clay, hovering over us, breathing into us his own divine life, smiling to see in us a reflection of himself. We go to our place of prayer confident that in prayer we transcend both place and time.

—JAMES FINLEY, *MERTON'S PALACE OF NOWHERE*

Prayer has far more to do with what God wants to do in us than with our trying to "reach" or "realize," still less "entertain," God in prayer. This truth eliminates anxiety and concern as to the success or nonsuccess of our prayer, for we can be quite certain that, if we want to pray and give the time to prayer, God is always successful and that is what matters. . . . What we think of as our search for God is, in reality, a response to the divine Lover drawing us to himself. There is never a moment when divine Love is not at work. . . . *This work is nothing other than a giving of the divine Self in love. The logical consequence for us must surely be that our part* is to let ourselves be loved, let ourselves be given to, let ourselves be worked upon by this great God and made capable of total union with Him.

—RUTH BURROWS, *ESSENCE OF PRAYER*

Week of Prayer #3: The Intimacy of Prayer

BECAUSE GOD CREATED US AND continues to create in and through us, we are by nature related to God. In other words, we are created in the image of God, and that image is indelible. The challenge for us is to be more aware of that ever-present relationship—which is hard to do in a world filled with many distractions.

This week we focus on prayer as intimate communication with God. As with any human relationship, we need to spend time together for that relationship to grow and deepen. Human relationships have different moments of greater and lesser intimacy—so, too, with God. Sometimes we are chatty, other times silent. Sometimes it's easy spending time with God; other times it's more difficult or taxing. There is no single way of relating to God, but as long as we are open, our relationship with God can grow in profound, sometimes unexpected ways.

† Prayer for the Week

I pray for the following graces: a deepening intimacy with God in prayer; a greater trust in God.

Day 1
Read Luke 11:1–13 ("Lord, teach us to pray"). Pray the Our Father slowly, letting the words sink in. Accept Jesus' invitation to ask for what you want.

Day 2

Read Isaiah 55:1–13 ("Incline your ear and come to me; listen, so that you may live"). Are you able to be still and simply listen to God, in Scripture and in the deepest desires of your heart?

Day 3

Read Psalm 63:1–8 ("My soul thirsts for you"). What do you thirst for? How do you experience God's "steadfast love"?

Day 4

Read Psalm 103 ("Bless the LORD, O my soul"). Speak a similar psalm from your heart.

Day 5

Read Romans 8:26–27. Prayer can be a struggle sometimes, but find consolation in the assurance that the Spirit helps us pray in our weakness. Where do you feel weak in your life now?

Day 6

Read Ephesians 3:14–21 (The power of Christ at work within us is able to accomplish more than we can ask or imagine). Where do you find that awesome power at work in your life? Where do you need such a divine, dynamic Presence?

Day 7

Review the week; savor the graces or return to a passage that was particularly meaningful for you.

The Saints Speak to Us about Prayer

True prayer is nothing but love.

—St. Augustine

Prayer is the inner bath of love into which the soul plunges itself.

—St. John Vianney

All of us must cling to God through prayer. My secret is simple: I pray. Through prayer I become one in love with Christ. I realize that praying to him is loving him. . . . In the silence of the heart God will speak.

—Mother Teresa of Calcutta

Everyone of us needs half an hour of prayer each day, except when we are busy—then we need an hour.

—St. Francis de Sales

Prayer is the raising of one's mind and heart to God or the requesting of good things from God.

—St. John Damascene

For me, prayer is a surge of the heart; it is a simple look turned toward heaven, it is a cry of recognition and of love, embracing both trial and joy.

—St. Thérèse of Lisieux

These quotes are compiled in the *United States Catholic Catechism for Adults.*

Distractions in Prayer

IT'S NATURAL TO BECOME DISTRACTED during prayer sometimes. If you can, simply acknowledge the distracting thought and let it go. Sometimes, however, what at first seems like a distraction offers an opportunity for a graced encounter with God. Thus, if the distracting thought continues, then carefully discern whether it's really a distraction or something you need to pray about.

In the course of a retreat in daily life, things happen at home, at work, or in relationships that beg for prayerful reflection. We should not hesitate to pray over the "scripture of our lives" if we think that God is trying to get our attention through what we initially thought was a distraction.

In contrast, some thoughts are really unnecessary preoccupations; we can tend to them later. Review the suggestions for preparing for and structuring your prayer time. Following these long-tested counsels can help focus your prayer. If distractions persist, talk with a spiritual director or guide about them. If you tend to fall asleep when you pray, adjust your posture or time of prayer.

Sometimes it can seem that nothing is happening, but deep down, God might be stirring up something—we just haven't realized it yet. As you grow in the habit of prayer, avoid the temptation to judge or rate your prayer: "Today was good prayer; yesterday was just OK." (Imagine rating each time you spent with a friend or loved one!) God can put anything to good use, even distractions and preoccupations.

In the end, heed the encouragement of St. Francis de Sales and others after him: If all you do is return to God's presence after distraction, then this is very good prayer. Your persistence shows how much you want to be with God.

Images of God

Fr. William A. Barry, SJ, a renowned spiritual director and scholar of the *Spiritual Exercises*, offers a very helpful, concise definition of prayer: *prayer is a conscious, personal relationship with God*. He proposes that we can learn about our relationship with God by considering our relationships with other people. In his book, *A Friendship Like No Other*, Fr. Barry refines his long-standing definition of prayer: "The best analogy for the relationship God wants with us is friendship. God desires humans into existence for the sake of friendship."

Barry's image of God's friendship may be novel to some, particularly those who wrestle with fearing God. We all have various images of God floating around in our heads. For example, because of our childhood experiences, we may see God as a kindly yet distant grandfather figure or as an accountant of good and bad deeds. Scripture gives us an assortment of images, including God as a nurturing mother; as a merciful Father; as a judge; as a benevolent Creator; as the Spirit; and of course, as Jesus Christ.

As we get older, our images of God evolve. You may encounter new images of God as you pray the Exercises. We need to let go of images that get in the way of a grown-up relationship with God, who is both far beyond us, yet so close to us.

No image fully captures who God is. We naturally try to put our experience of God into words, but all words will be inadequate because we are dealing with God, who is Ultimate Mystery. We must be careful not to turn our images of God into idols. Instead, we let God reveal Godself to us, gently and naturally.

If you experience God as mostly removed from your life, or if you commonly have feelings of fear when approaching God, then you may want to take extra time with these introductory days of the Exercises, praying your way to a more trusting experience of God. The writer of the first letter of John assures us, "There is no fear in love, but perfect love casts out fear" (4:18). Pray to experience such consoling love of God, who deeply desires for us to experience the joy of our creation.

Week of Prayer #4: God's Invitation to Greater Freedom

One of the goals of the Spiritual Exercises is to help retreatants grow in spiritual freedom. In Ignatius's words, the Exercises are intended "to overcome oneself and to order one's life, without reaching a decision through some disordered affection" (*SE* 21).

Spiritual freedom is an interior freedom, a freedom of the mind and heart. People who are spiritually free know who they are—with all of their gifts and limitations—and are comfortable with who they are. They are able to discern God's presence; find meaning in their lives, and make choices that flow from who they are, whatever the circumstance. In his oft-quoted study of the Exercises, *Spiritual Freedom*, John J. English, SJ, describes this freedom as an "acceptance of oneself as historically coming from God, going to God, and being with God" (p. 18).

With this reminder of our most fundamental identity, we keep God at the center of our lives. We work at becoming more aware of God's call in our lives and to responding generously to that call. We have numerous preoccupations that get in the way of our hearing and responding to God's call: fears, prejudices, greed, the need to control, perfectionism, jealousies, resentments, and excessive self-doubts. These tendencies bind us and hold us back from loving God, ourselves, and others as we ought to. They create chaos in our souls and lead us to make poor choices.

Lacking spiritual freedom, we become excessively attached to persons, places, material possessions, titles, occupations, honors, and the acclaim of others. These things are good in themselves when ordered and directed by the love of God. They become **disordered attachments** or **disordered loves** when they push God out of the center of our lives and become key to our identity. As these weeks of prayer have emphasized, the fundamental truth of our identity is that God loves us unconditionally.

This week, we pray for greater spiritual freedom. In so doing, we become aware of our disordered attachments. Such self-examination will continue in the weeks ahead, so do not feel pressure to get your house in order all in one week. Let God's liberating grace gently work on you.

✝ Prayer for the Week

I pray for the following graces: to grow in interior freedom; to become more aware of disordered attachments that get in the way of loving God, others, or myself.

Day 1
Read Luke 1:26–38. Pray over the story of the Annunciation and marvel at Mary's freedom to say, "Yes!" Notice how she deals with her fears and keeps her focus on God. Pray over the words of the Gospel slowly, meditatively, or use your imagination to place yourself in the scene.

Day 2
Repetition of Luke 1:26–38 (see following material "Ignatian Repetition" for an explanation of repetition).

Day 3
Read Mark 10:17–27 (Jesus calls the rich man to follow him). Consider the rich man's spiritual freedom or lack thereof. Notice how Jesus relates to him. Ask: *What attracts me to following Jesus, and what holds me back?*

DAY 4

Repetition of Mark 10:17–27.

DAY 5

Read Philippians 3:7–16. Pray for St. Paul's single-minded and single-hearted focus on Christ. Ask: *When have I experienced or witnessed such focus, such freedom in my life?* We always need to pray for more spiritual freedom; we cannot become free on our own.

DAY 6

Read John 3:22–30. Reflect on John the Baptist's freedom: "He must increase, but I must decrease." *How have I demonstrated such freedom and other-centeredness? Where in my life do I still need to let go of excessive self-preoccupation and control?*

DAY 7

Review the week; savor the graces.

For Further Reflection

O Spirit of God,
we ask you to help orient
all our actions by your inspirations,
carry them on by your gracious assistance,
that every prayer and work of ours
may always begin from you
and through you
be happily ended.
Amen.

This prayer for spiritual freedom has often been used by Jesuits to begin classes or meetings.

Ignatian Repetition

GIVEN IGNATIUS'S ANALOGY OF SPIRITUAL exercise (or prayer) to physical exercise, we may be tempted to race through the Spiritual Exercises. However, to grow in prayer means that we do not skim the surface but go ever deeper into the mystery of God. At the beginning of the Exercises, Ignatius reminds us that what satisfies the soul is not knowing more facts or reaching great insights, but savoring the many graces of God and resting in the Divine Presence (*SE* 2). In other words, in the spiritual life we try to go deeper rather than spread ourselves too thin.

To help us simplify and slow down our praying, Ignatius suggests that we do "repetitions" of previous exercises (*SE* 62). This doesn't mean that we reenact a prayer period minute by minute or rehearse every part of the exercise or Scripture passage. Instead, we return to some word, image, desire, insight, feeling, attraction, resistance, or other interior movement that was particularly strong when we first prayed that exercise.

Repetitions are not meant to be boring, as if to say, "I've already done that!" Instead, they are intended to simplify our prayer and help us go deeper. Making a repetition of prayer is like spending more time with someone we love.

A Prayer by St. Anselm of Canterbury

Teach me to seek you,
and reveal yourself to me as I seek;
for unless you instruct me
I cannot seek you,
and unless you reveal yourself
I cannot find you.
Let me seek you in desiring you;
let me desire you in seeking you.
Let me find you in loving you;
let me love you in finding you.

St. Anselm (1033–1109) lived as a monk and later served as the Archbishop of Canterbury. An eminent theologian, Anselm proposed the classic definition of theology as "faith seeking understanding."

WEEK OF PRAYER #5: THE PRINCIPLE AND FOUNDATION

So far in the retreat, we have remembered God's faithfulness to us and have savored God's unconditional, boundless love for us and all of creation. Filled with gratitude, we respond most naturally by loving in return. All we want is to praise, love, and serve God, and we will do anything or make whatever sacrifices necessary to fulfill this most fundamental human calling, or vocation.

Such holy desires are at the core of the first key meditation of the Exercises, the **Principle and Foundation**. It reads like a mission statement for the human person: "I am created to praise, love, and serve God." Of course, this vocation is specified in each unique human life. When we live out of this vocation, we are truly happy and fulfilled. When we allow disordered loves and self-preoccupations to clutter our lives, we find ourselves out of balance, unhappy, and discontented.

The grace we seek is **indifference**. In Ignatian vocabulary, this term does not mean an unfeeling lack of concern. Instead, indifference means that we hold all of God's gifts reverently, gratefully, but also lightly, embracing them or letting them go, all depending on how they help us fulfill our vocation to love in everyday, concrete details.

Indifference is another way of describing spiritual freedom. It is a stance of openness to God: we look for God in any person, any situation, and any moment. Indifference means that we are free to love and serve as God desires. Spiritual freedom or indifference is a gift from God; we can't make it happen. But we can, over time, foster indifference by developing good habits of thinking, choosing, and acting.

The Principle and Foundation is densely worded, but it is not meant to be an academic exercise. Consider it an invitation for you to experience more deeply how intimately related you are to God and to all of God's creation (including persons, other creatures, and the natural world). In so doing, certain fundamental truths about our existence come alive: God creates me out of love, in a particular time and place, with particular talents and temperaments, strengths and limitations. God continues to create and to reveal who God is to me and who I am before God. God invites me to partner with God to build a more just and gentle world. I learn that the best way to praise God is to be who God made me to be and to honor the uniqueness of other creatures.

Our appreciation of the Principle and Foundation deepens as we move through the Exercises and as we try to integrate that understanding into daily life. What may begin as a mental exercise seeps into the heart as we progress in the retreat.

✝ Prayer for the Week

I pray for the following graces: a deepening awareness of my fundamental vocation to praise, love, and serve God and others; a desire for greater indifference in my life; a willingness to embrace who I am before our loving God.

Day 1

Prayerfully read the *traditional* translation of the Principle and Foundation that follows. Ask: *How do I concretely praise, love, and serve God? What activities, people, or material things help me achieve this end?*

DAY 2

Prayerfully read the *contemporary* translation of the Principle and Foundation that follows. Ask: *How have I been a "good steward" of the gifts God has given me, including created things, my talents, and my abilities? From my own experience, what gets in the way of my praising, loving, and serving God? How do the following influence my choices and actions: titles, honors, possessions, career, opinion of others, lifestyle?* Be as concrete as possible.

DAY 3

Read Exodus 3:1–15. Consider how God calls Moses to partner with God in the work of liberation: "I will send you to Pharaoh to bring my people, the Israelites, out of Egypt." Reflect on your own life: *How have I partnered with God to help people, to build a more just and gentle world, to care for creation?*

DAY 4

Repetition. As you consider again Ignatius's Principle and Foundation, recall moments in your life when you felt in balance and times when you felt out of balance. In other words, recall times of great spiritual freedom and moments of spiritual chaos. Whom do you look up to as people living in spiritual freedom?

DAY 5

In the light of your prayer over the past three days, write out the Principle and Foundation in your own words—that is, write out the mission statement that you want to govern your life. Or create an image reflecting your Principle and Foundation (see, for example, Jeremiah 17:5–11).

DAY 6

Read Philippians 4:11–13 ("I can do all things through him who strengthens me"). Continue working on your own

Principle and Foundation. You may note the disordered attachments or "unfreedoms" in your life that are roadblocks in your spiritual journey. Remember, we always need God's help to experience the spiritual freedom we desire.

Day 7
Review the week; savor the graces.

Principle and Foundation: Traditional Translation

HUMAN BEINGS ARE CREATED TO praise, reverence, and serve God our Lord, and by means of doing this to save their souls.

The other things on the face of the earth are created for the human beings, to help them in the pursuit of the end for which they are created.

From this it follows that we ought to use these things to the extent that they help us toward our end, and free ourselves from them to the extent that they hinder us from it.

To attain this it is necessary to make ourselves indifferent to all created things, in regard to everything which is left to our free will and is not forbidden. Consequently, on our own part we ought not to seek health rather than sickness, wealth rather than poverty, honor rather than dishonor, a long life rather than a short one, and so on in all other matters.

Rather, we ought to desire and choose only that which is more conducive to the end for which we are created (*SE* 23).

Translation by George E. Ganss, SJ, *The Spiritual Exercises of Saint Ignatius.*

Principle and Foundation: Contemporary Translation

GOD WHO LOVES US CREATES us and wants to share life with us forever. Our love response takes shape in our praise and honor and service of the God of our life.

All the things in this world are also created because of God's love and they become a context of gifts, presented to us so that we can know God more easily and make a return of love more readily.

As a result, we show reverence for all the gifts of creation and collaborate with God in using them so that by being good stewards we develop as loving persons in our care for God's world and its development. But if we abuse any of these gifts of creation or, on the contrary, take them as the center of our lives, we break our relationship with God and hinder our growth as loving persons.

In everyday life, then, we must hold ourselves in balance before all created gifts insofar as we have a choice and are not bound by some responsibility. We should not fix our desires on health or sickness, wealth or poverty, success or failure, a long life or a short one. For everything has the potential of calling forth in us a more loving response to our life forever with God.

Our only desire and our one choice should be this: I want and I choose what better leads to God's deepening life in me (*SE* 23).

Translation by David L. Fleming, SJ, in *Draw Me into Your Friendship: The Spiritual Exercises—A Literal Translation and a Contemporary Reading.*

For Further Reflection

It is true to say that for me sanctity consists in being myself and for you sanctity consists in being your self and that, in the last analysis, your sanctity will never be mine and mine will never be yours, except in the communism of charity and grace.

For me to be a saint means to be myself. Therefore the problem of sanctity and salvation is in fact the problem of finding out who I am and of discovering my true self.

—THOMAS MERTON, *NEW SEEDS OF CONTEMPLATION*

Week of Prayer #6: God's Call to Me

Only when we are really free can we hear God's call. This week, we reflect on how God calls us right now in the concrete particulars of our lives. Do not worry about making big decisions or changing the way you live. That may come later. Instead, simply marvel that God calls each of us specially. Listen not only to the call but also to the One who calls.

We encounter God in a variety of ways: in the people around us and in the work we are doing; in something we read or see in the world; and in the inspiration of Scripture and the church's liturgy. We also find God in the holy desires brewing deep in our hearts. This is a central insight to Ignatian spirituality. Because God, our Creator, gives us life and because we are the image of God, God's desires and our deepest desires are one and the same. What we truly desire is also what God desires for us. Discerning these desires takes practice. As the retreat progresses, Ignatius offers tools for discernment, which we will review.

God is always trying to get our attention in ways both obvious and subtle. We are reminded of the prophet Elijah who, standing on a mountaintop, found God not in a mighty wind, or in an earthquake, or in fire, but in a "sound of sheer silence" (1 Kings 19:11–13). We can find God in the busyness of our lives and in the silence of our prayer.

✝ Prayer for the Week

I pray for the following grace: a grateful awareness of the many ways in which God calls me.

Day 1

Read Mark 10:46–52. Hear Jesus say to the blind man: "What do want me to do for you?" Hear Jesus say the same to you. What is your heartfelt response?

Day 2

Read Jeremiah 1:4–10 (call of Jeremiah). Ask: *How do I react to God's call in my life?*

Day 3

Read Jeremiah 29:11–14 ("I know the plans I have for you"). As you consider the retreat ahead, or your life ahead, rest in the assurance of God's faithful presence.

Day 4

Repetition of any day.

Day 5

Read Luke 5:1–11 (call of the disciples by the shore). Listen to Jesus telling Simon Peter, and you, "Do not be afraid." Ask: *Where do I experience God calling me in the midst of my daily life?*

Day 6

Read John 1:35–39. Listen to Jesus say to the disciples, and to you: "What are you looking for?" How do you respond?

Day 7

Repetition of any day. Savor the graces of the week.

Praying

It doesn't have to be
the blue iris, it could be
weeds in a vacant lot, or a few
small stones; just
pay attention, then patch

a few words together and don't try
to make them elaborate, this isn't
a contest but the doorway

into thanks, and a silence in which
another voice may speak.

—MARY OLIVER, *THIRST: POEMS BY MARY OLIVER*

A Prayer by John Henry Cardinal Newman

God has created me to do Him some definite service;
He has committed some work to me
which He has not committed to another.
I have my mission—
I may never know it in this life, but I shall be told it in the next.
. . . I am a link in a chain,
a bond of connection between persons.

He has not created me for naught.
I shall do good;
I shall do His work;
I shall be an angel of peace,
a preacher of truth in my own place, while not intending it,
if I do but keep his Commandments.

... Therefore I will trust Him.
Whatever, wherever I am.
I can never be thrown away.

If I am in sickness, my sickness may serve Him;
in perplexity, my perplexity may serve Him;
in sorrow, my sorrow may serve Him.

... He does nothing in vain.
... He knows what He is about.

JOHN HENRY NEWMAN (1801–1890) was a preeminent Christian thinker and apologist of his time. Newman published and lectured widely on an assortment of topics, such as the development of Christian doctrine, conscience, ecumenism, the role of the laity, and Catholic university education. First as an Anglican clergy and later as a Catholic priest, Newman cared deeply about the spiritual formation of people and tried to blend his roles as theologian and pastor. He was declared venerable by Pope John Paul II in 1991 and beatified by Pope Benedict XVI in 2010.

St. Ignatius's Prayer of Awareness: The Examen

St. Ignatius believed that we can find God in all things, at every moment, even in the most ordinary times. To do this, we must take time to reflect on our experience, to look at the data of a day and discern their meaning. Ignatius encourages us to look back over a period of time and pay attention to what is happening in and around us. Then he invites us to look ahead, to what comes next, so that we can act in a way worthy of our vocation as Christians. A daily practice of praying the Examen (perhaps for about ten or fifteen minutes) helps us discern how God is calling us in small and large ways. God is found in what is real, so we pray from what is real in our lives. Over the centuries, the Examen has been adapted in different ways. I have broken down this daily prayer into five steps. Do not feel that you need to do all five steps or use a precise formula of words. This is not about completing a task but about building a relationship.

What follows is a general overview of those five steps.

1. Pray for God's Help

There is nothing magical about praying. Prayer is a conversation with God. So invite God to be with you during this sacred time. Ask God to help you be grateful and honest as you look back on the day. With God's help, be attentive to how the Spirit was working in and through you, others, and creation. Let yourself see your day as God sees it.

2. Give Thanks for the Gifts of This Day

For Ignatius, gratitude is the first, most important step on the spiritual journey. An attitude of gratitude, practiced often enough, helps us find God in all things and can transform the way we look at our life and at other people.

So review the day and name the blessings, from the most significant and obvious to the more common and ordinary. God (*not* the devil) is found in the details, so be very specific! As you take stock, honor the gifts of others in your life, but don't forget to recognize the gifts in you, for they, too, are God given.

Don't feel that you must mechanically go through the day hour by hour or make a list of *all* the day's gifts. Instead, savor whatever gifts God shows you. With God's gentle guidance, *let the day go through you.*

3. Pray over the Significant Feelings That Surface as You Replay the Day

Ignatius believed that God communicates with us not only through mental insight but also through our "interior movements," as he called them: our feelings, emotions, desires, attractions, repulsions, and moods. As you reflect on the day, you may notice some strong feelings arise. They may be painful or pleasing—for example, joy, peace, sadness, anxiety, confusion, hope, compassion, regret, anger, confidence, jealousy, self-doubt, boredom, or excitement.

Feelings are neither positive nor negative: it is what you do with them that raises moral questions. These movements can tell you about the direction of your life on this specific day. And simply bringing them to the surface can help release the destructive hold that some feelings have on you.

Pick one or two strong feelings or movements and pray from them. Ask God to help you understand what aroused those feelings and where they led you:

- Did they draw you closer to God? Did they help you grow in faith, hope, and love? Did they make you more generous with your time and talent? Did they make you feel more alive, whole, and human? Did they lead you to feel more connected to others or challenge you to life-giving growth?

- Or did the feelings lead you away from God, make you less faithful, hopeful, and loving? Did they cause you to become more self-centered or anxious? Did they lure you into doubt and confusion? Did they lead to the breakdown of relationships?

4. Rejoice and Seek Forgiveness

Rejoice in those times that you were brought closer to God, and ask forgiveness for those times today when you resisted God's presence in your life. Praise God for the grace of awareness given to you during this time of prayer, even if you became aware of things you are not proud of. This awareness is the beginning of healing and conversion.

5. Look to Tomorrow

Just as God is with you today, God will be with you as you sleep and when you wake up tomorrow. Invite God to be a part of your future. What do you need God's help with? Be very practical and specific. If it's helpful, look at your schedule for tomorrow. God wants to be there with you, in the most dramatic and mundane moments of your life. Ask God to give you the grace you need—for example, courage, confidence, wisdom, patience, determination, or peace. Or perhaps there is someone you would like to pray for by name.

Close by speaking to God from your heart or with a prayer that is familiar to you, such as the Our Father.

The "First Week"

†

Experiencing the Boundless Mercy of God

AFTER MY TWO-YEAR NOVITIATE AND upon professing vows of poverty, chastity, and obedience, I was sent to study philosophy and theology at Fordham University. The summer after my first year, I asked to go to Bolivia to enrich my Spanish and to live with the Jesuits there. I really needed to work on my Spanish, I explained. And I wanted to get to know the Jesuits and their work in South America. All good reasons, my superiors responded, "but we are going to send you to India to work in a leprosy hospital."

India? A leprosy hospital?

Such is the vow of obedience, I learned. Sometimes my religious superiors have a better idea than I do about what I need. As I flew halfway around the world with two other Jesuit scholastics, Tim and James, I wondered what the point of this experience was. It didn't take long to find out. I had to be schooled in a way far different from how I was learning in graduate school.

John's looming figure greeted us at the hot, crowded airport in Calcutta (now known as Kolkata). A native of Baltimore, John considered northeast India home after having lived there as a Jesuit priest for nearly fifty years. Six and a half feet tall with a ruddy Irish complexion and a smile wider than the distance we had traveled, John certainly stood out in the crowd. "Welcome to paradise," he said. We were exhausted from a long journey and anxious about what was coming next. We spent a night catching up on sleep at a local Jesuit community that served one of the countless schools named after the great Jesuit missionary saint, Francis Xavier. The next day, John drove us up to Dhanbad, a small city two hours northwest of Calcutta.

What I noticed first were the cows, blackened from the coal dust that filled the heavy air. Dhanbad was the site of several coal mines. The companies strip-mined, raking the earth to find the coal beneath and leaving behind an environmental mess. Thus, it was a relief when John took us to our home for the summer a few miles outside of Dhanbad, to the Nirmala Hospital. The hospital was founded in 1969 by Jesuit missionaries from our part of the United States. Surrounded by a wall and natural leafy vegetation, the hospital grounds were an oasis of serenity and cleanliness. The religious sisters (mainly Samaritan Sisters) from southern India maintained a soothing order to the property.

On its fifty acres, Nirmala was more than a hospital; it was a small village. It featured dormitories where as many as 140 patients slept in several one-room buildings, their beds lined up in long rows. The hospital building itself was more like a clinic, where very rudimentary care was given with the limited supplies at hand. A chapel, a convent for the sisters, and a small rectory for priests were reminders of Nirmala's religious mission. The goal was not to convert the mostly Hindu patients but to live the gospel in a very real way by responding to the needs of the poorest of the poor. In India today, those with leprosy (or Hansen's disease, as it is medically known) still suffer from discrimination and are pushed to the margins of society. Although the disease is 100 percent curable with a months-long regime of oral medications, the poor often lack access to the medications or information about infection and treatment. Because they are malnourished, their immune systems are not able to fight the bacterium that causes the disease. In overcrowded living quarters and unsanitary conditions, the disease is easily transmitted.

Because children of leprosy patients suffer social stigma along with their parents, Nirmala included a school. In the back of the compound, a series of bungalows were arranged in a square with a central courtyard. These simple, concrete structures housed former patients who could not find work or a home. Though cured of the leprosy, they still bore the painful marks of the disease: blindness, a clenched fist, a flattened nose, or amputated limbs. It was to this part of Nirmala that John first took us for our official welcome. We were greeted by singing and dancing. At the center of the celebration was an elderly blind man who had stumps for feet and relied on his crutches to move about.

As the days wore on, the initial excitement of our adventure receded and the boredom crept in. Life moved at a slow pace in Nirmala, especially amid the frequent power outages. The stifling heat and humidity slowed our pace even more. There was not much to do, at least compared with what we left back home in the States. We were awake with the sun (and roosters) and attended Mass with the few Catholics who lived at Nirmala. After a simple breakfast, we spent the mornings taking patients in wheelchairs from the dormitories to the clinic, where their bandages were replaced, or to the rehabilitation room, where they learned to regain some dexterity in their arms and hands.

We spent afternoons at the school trying to teach a little English to the Hindi-speaking children. We were a novelty to the hundred or so children there. In the evenings, John entertained James, Tim, and me with countless tales of his life in India. He did this in part to pass the time but also to encourage us among the challenges of life in a less developed country. John had a contagious sense of humor. When the power ran out or when the food ran low or when the heat dragged us all down, he often quoted Scripture to us, with a smile: "The trials of this life, boys, are nothing in comparison to the joys that await us in heaven!"

In the first two weeks, the life at Nirmala began to take a toll on me—the heat, the food, the boredom, the bugs, the snakes, the power outages. In addition to our simple living, I felt more and more frustrated at not being able to communicate with the patients in their various tribal languages. The language barrier seemed insurmountable. I was being trained for ministry as a priest, yet I was stripped of the ability to rely on the spoken word to console patients. I felt useless. As I mutely went about my work, I wondered why I had come eight thousand miles to push wheelchairs all morning and entertain schoolchildren who couldn't understand anything I said.

Sensing my growing desolation—and probably tired of my complaining—John gently but firmly counseled me: "Kevin, let them teach you something. Remember the risen Lord appeared to his disciples with the marks of the crucifixion still in his hands and feet. With their crippled hands and feet, they bring you the Lord. They have something to show you." Humbled, I began to let go and waited on the Lord. I was ready to be schooled.

Sona was one of my first teachers. Thirteen years old, she was the youngest in the twenty-five-bed women's ward. She had been at the hospital for more than a year, an unusually long period of time. During those lonely months, no one had come to visit her. In those first weeks, when I came into the dormitory with my rickety wheelchair, many women would stand up at their beds at once and try to get my attention with words I didn't understand. I did not know how to ask in Hindi such simple questions as, "Who goes first?" In the ensuing chaos, Sona would laugh mischievously. I was completely perplexed.

One day though, I came in, but the usual confusion didn't greet me. From her bed, Sona had organized who would go first and next, pointing one after the other. She always saved herself for last. I learned to say "thank you" to her in Hindi. But I wanted to do more than that. So one day, while pushing Sona to the clinic, I picked one of the beautiful purple flowers that graced the pathway to the clinic and put it in her hair. Her always-radiant smile widened even more.

In a world that deems someone untouchable, I slowly learned the power of human touch, a simple gesture that communicates unfathomable dignity. When approached by someone pleading to be healed, Jesus sometimes relied, not on the power of his spoken word alone, but on the simple human gesture of touch. Reaching out, Jesus made them whole again, not just physically whole but also spiritually and socially. Having been ostracized in the past, they left Jesus accepted, an outcast no longer.

Gradually, I became more comfortable lifting patients from their beds and placing my hands on theirs. When I met Suken, his illness was so advanced that he was sequestered in a closetlike room because the smell of his deteriorating flesh was so strong. Nothing remained of his hands and feet. Blindness had already set in, and as the cartilage in his nose deteriorated, his face seemed to cave in on itself. When I picked him up to put him in the wheelchair, he weighed no more than seventy-five pounds. He was one of the few who died in the hospital; we buried him in a cemetery behind the hospital shortly before I left. Over the years, patients were buried at random angles, in the same anonymity with which they lived their lives as lepers. Mounds of dirt overgrown with grass and weeds marked the graves.

With a fortified immune system, there was no danger of my contracting leprosy. All that prevented me from engaging the patients on a human level was my own awkward feeling of difference—and sometimes, I'm embarrassed to admit, my repulsion at the physical deformity I saw and smelled. At Nirmala, however, with all the usual clutter and comforts of my life removed, there was little to divide us. I learned that sometimes words are not enough and that each of us needs at times a healing, human touch.

John and my new "teachers" at Nirmala schooled me in solidarity, the virtue that recognizes that we belong to one another and must look out for one another. Amid our many differences, solidarity points to our shared human needs and longings. Such a perspective means that when we serve someone, we are also served by that person. In this relationship of mutuality, we both learn and grow, although perhaps in different ways.

Embracing relationships or networks of solidarity is ultimately liberating. I began to enjoy my time at Nirmala. I learned not to mind being made fun of by the schoolchildren—it was their way of relating to this strange man who was living with them. I became more playful with them, one day unleashing a barrage of water balloons on an unsuspecting mass of children. I finally accepted the invitation to play soccer in the cow pasture behind the hospital grounds (which turned very interesting when the monsoon rains came). From the elderly for whom Nirmala was a permanent home, I enjoyed a hospitality I had not experienced before, as they welcomed me into their small living space and shared with me what little they had. Blood relations meant little; everyone was family. Still untrained in their language, I learned to listen with my eyes.

In the frequent downtime, John, Tim, James, and I spent countless hours together talking, laughing, and praying together. We needed one another to stay healthy and to work through the challenges we faced. We learned to speak from the heart in the way we had not before. Gone were the natural competitive streaks of men of our age. We laughed more easily together.

At Nirmala, I learned how narrow was my vision and how closed was my heart. I confronted some painful realities about myself. I noticed how trapped I had become by the materialism of my culture. Even with my vow of poverty, I had filled my life with so many things, which only put up barriers between me and other people. I prized my independence, but at Nirmala, I learned how I had made individualism an idol. I became more vulnerable to my Jesuit brothers and to my new friends at Nirmala. Although I came from privilege, I learned that I was poor in many ways, building a false sense of security on things, on reputation, on being productive and seemingly perfect, and on performing to meet others' expectations. Back in the States, I was always rushing, always trying to do something or outdo someone else, which left little time simply to be and to enjoy the grace of the moment. Finally, I learned how much of a disordered priority I put on physical appearance—my own and that of others. Leprosy and poverty can ravage a human body, but they cannot touch the beauty of the person inside.

In short, I came to embrace my own weakness and sin, which left more room for God and others to give me strength. I had come halfway around the world to experience more fully a freedom I had tasted when first making the thirty-day Spiritual Exercises more than a year before. Then, I honestly reckoned with this history of sin in my life. In the **First Week** of the Exercises, we meet a faithful and loving God who broadens our vision and breaks open our heart. This merciful God seeks only to liberate us from anything that gets in the way of loving ourselves, others, and God—that is, from anything that makes us truly unhappy. All of those lessons came alive again at Nirmala.

On my last day there, I made the rounds saying my good-byes. My last stop was the "retirement community" in the back of the compound. There I saw one of the grandmothers sitting in a rocking chair on her porch. Playing at her feet was a young girl, laughing. A middle-aged woman stood behind the chair, gracefully brushing the grandmother's long, graying hair in deliberate strokes, because she had no hands with which to do it herself. I waved good-bye and turned away, realizing why I was sent to India and this most amazing school of the heart.

A Prayer by Pierre Teilhard de Chardin, SJ

Above all, trust in the slow work of God.

We are quite naturally impatient in everything,
to reach the end without delay.
We should like to skip the intermediate stages.
We are impatient of being on the way
to something unknown,
something new.

And yet it is the law of all progress
that it is made by passing through
some stages of instability—
and that it may take a very long time.

And so I think it is with you;
your ideas mature gradually—let them grow,
let them shape themselves, without undue haste.
Don't try to force them on,
as though you could be today what time
(that is to say, grace and circumstances
acting on your own good will)
will make of you tomorrow.

Only God could say what this new spirit
gradually forming within you will be.
Give Our Lord the benefit of believing
that his hand is leading you,
and accept the anxiety of feeling yourself
in suspense, and incomplete.

Pierre Teilhard de Chardin, SJ (1881–1955), was a French Jesuit priest, theologian, and paleontologist. In his prolific writings, he tried to integrate theology, science, and spirituality. His mystical vision of the world, which considered matter and spirit a unified reality, has captured the imagination of believers for decades.

WEEK OF PRAYER #7:
THE REALITY OF SIN

THIS WEEK, WE BEGIN WHAT Ignatius calls the **First Week** of his Exercises. By "week," Ignatius does not mean seven calendar days, but a particular movement or phase of the retreat. Most broadly, the First Week focuses on our experience of sin—personally, communally, and globally. Sin can be described in many ways: as a breakdown of a relationship with God and others; as a failure to love God, others, and self; as a turning away from God.

Sin is an inescapable reality of the human condition; we abuse the freedom God gives us and make choices that hurt God, others, and ourselves. God does not punish us for our sins; instead, we suffer the natural consequences that flow from our sinful choices and the sinful choices of others. We see the effects of sin in the disorder of our individual lives and in social structures that dehumanize, marginalize, oppress, and hurt people.

In the meditations that follow, Ignatius proposes that we look at the history of sin in an epic, panoramic way. We consider the cosmic battle between good and evil and watch how it plays out in every human heart. Because we can sometimes deceive ourselves or be blind to our own human frailty, we ask God to reveal to us our sins. Our aim is not to become mired in guilt, self-hate, or despair. Instead, we ask for a healthy sense of shame and confusion when confronting the reality of sin. Knowing how good God is to us, how and why do we still choose to sin, still choose to respond so meagerly to God's generosity?

Even as we recognize these hard realities, we remember the graces of the past few weeks of prayer. Particularly, we recall that God loves us unconditionally and wants to free us from anything that blocks our growing into the people God calls us to be. We don't get very far just by counting our sins and trying to overcome them by sheer force of will. Instead, we need to keep our eyes fixed on God's ever-present mercy, which is the ultimate source of our lasting liberation from sin.

We seek healing. Just as bodily healing often begins with some physical pain, healing of the soul begins with a graced awareness of our disordered loves and self-preoccupations.

✝ Prayer for the Week

I pray for the following grace: a healthy sense of shame and confusion before God as I consider the effects of sin in my life, my community, and my world.

Day 1

Read Luke 15:11–32 (The parable of the prodigal son and his brother). Consider: *How does Jesus' parable help me understand my own estrangement from God and others? How does it help me appreciate God's welcome to me, a sinner?* In this parable, Jesus tells us who the Father is. Notice that the father in the parable is also prodigal—that is, extravagant—with his love. God is always trying to overcome separation. Notice the festivity of the parable. Realize how much joy it brings God when we return home.

Day 2

To deepen our understanding of the nature of sin and its effects, Ignatius proposes a **meditation on the sin of the angels**. In the Christian tradition, Satan and his minions were the first to reject God's love. This failure to praise and honor God the Creator had cosmic implications. Although there are few biblical references to the fall of the angels (see, for example, Luke 10:18: "I watched Satan fall from heaven like a flash of lightning"), theological reflection and the Christian imagination (such as in art and literature) have informed our understanding of evil's reality.

The bottom line is that the angels, as creatures of God, enjoyed the gift of freedom and were given a choice. Some of these pure spirits chose to put themselves before God, rejecting God's love and God's offer to share in divine life. These angels could not stand it when God chose to become like us (not them), taking the form of a human being in Jesus Christ. For our prayer, Ignatius suggests the following:

> I will call to memory the sin of the angels: how they were created in grace and then, not wanting to better themselves by using their freedom to reverence and obey their Creator and Lord, they fell into pride, were changed from grace to malice, and were hurled from heaven into hell. (*SE* 50)

Spend some time considering the radical choice of the angels. Use your imagination. Feel God's sadness at this rebellion. Consider the angels' self-isolation. Recall your own rebellions, those times when you have chosen self before God.

Day 3

Continuing this reflection on the history of sin, Ignatius moves us to a **meditation on the sin of Adam and Eve** (*SE* 51). Biblical scholarship has long held that the story of Adam and Eve in the book of Genesis is not history but a theological reflection by the people of Israel on the reality of good and evil. This story speaks a timeless truth known to all humanity: human beings, like the angels, enjoy the gift of freedom, yet we sometimes choose to abuse that freedom by trying to put ourselves at the center of creation and displacing God. This is the essence of original sin.

Prayerfully read the story of Adam and Eve, Cain and Abel (Genesis 2:4–4:16). What do you learn about the nature of sin and the effects of sin? Notice how subtle evil can be and how alluring the temptation to avoid responsibility. Consider some of your own sinful choices. In your journal, note any emotional responses to your considerations of sin.

Rev. Michael Himes of Boston College has an interesting take on this age-old story. The first chapter of Genesis tells us that human beings were created in the image and likeness of God and that God called our creation very good. The temptation of Adam and Eve is to disbelieve that good news and refuse to accept our innate goodness and the goodness of others. Instead, they think that they must do something else to become like God or become valuable in God's eyes. Consider all the evil effects that flow from not accepting the inherent goodness and dignity of each person.

Day 4

The cosmic battle between good and evil is played out in each person's heart. Ignatius offers a final consideration of sin: **the sin of one person** who chooses definitively against God (*SE 52*).

Prayerfully read Luke 16:19–31, the parable of the rich man and Lazarus. How does Jesus' parable help you understand what sin is and how it affects us? What would it be like for a person to be totally closed off from God's love? You may want to craft a parable of your own, replacing the rich man and Lazarus with modern-day counterparts based on the current century's sad history of sin, violence, genocide, and injustice.

Ask: *When have I failed to notice or respond to the needs of others? When have I felt isolated from God or others by my own sin?*

Day 5

Read Romans 5:1–11 ("God proves his love for us in that while we still were sinners Christ died for us"). Now use your imagination to place yourself before Jesus on the cross, which is a reminder of God's faithfulness and mercy. You may want to meditate on an artistic rendering of the familiar scene at Calvary. Follow Ignatius's instructions (*SE* 53):

> Imagine Christ our Lord suspended on the cross before you, and converse with him in a colloquy: How is it is that he, although he is the Creator, has come to make himself a human being? How is it that he has passed from eternal life to death here in time, and to die in this way for my sins?
>
> In a similar way, reflect on yourself and ask:
>
> What have I done for Christ?
>
> What am I doing for Christ?
>
> What ought I do for Christ?
>
> In this way, too, gazing on him in so pitiful a state as he hangs on the cross, speak out whatever comes to your mind.

For more explanation of what Ignatius means by a "colloquy," see the chapter that follows.

Day 6
Repetition of the parable of the prodigal son and his brother. Conclude with the colloquy from Day 5.

Day 7
Review the week as a whole and savor the graces. Conclude with the colloquy from Day 5.

The Colloquy

IGNATIUS SUGGESTS THAT WE INCLUDE a "colloquy" in each of these meditations on sin and in later exercises as well (*SE* 53–54). A colloquy is an intimate conversation between you and God the Father, between you and Jesus, or between you and Mary or one of the saints. It often occurs at the end of a prayer period, but it can take place at any time. Let this conversation naturally develop in your prayer.

In the colloquy, we speak and listen as the Spirit moves us: expressing ourselves, for example,

> as a friend speaks to a friend, or
>
> as a person speaks to one whom he or she has offended, or
>
> as a child speaks to a parent or mentor, or
>
> as a lover speaks to his or her beloved.

Whatever the context, be "real," speaking from the heart. As in any meaningful conversation, make sure to leave times of silence for listening.

In the meditations on sin, Ignatius suggests that we place ourselves before the cross and consider three questions that echo throughout the Exercises:

What have I done for Christ?

What am I doing for Christ?

What ought I do for Christ?

Return to these questions throughout the retreat. In one sense, they are not completely answerable during the retreat itself; we often lean into the answers as we continue our normal routines. By considering the questions, we realize how practical the Exercises are. Just as our sin is reflected in concrete decisions and actions, so, too, does grace come to life in choices and deeds for the love of Christ and others. We encounter Christ not only in our prayer and in the sacraments but also in our relationships with the Body of Christ, living now as the church, the people of God.

For Further Reflection

Prayer is a matter of relationship. Intimacy is the basic issue, not answers to problems or resolutions "to be better." Many of life's problems and challenges have no answers; we can only live with and through them. Problems and challenges, however, can be faced and lived through with more peace and resilience if people know that they are not alone. A man's wife will not return from the dead, but the pain is more bearable when he has poured out his sorrow, his anger, and his despair to God and has experienced God's intimate presence.

—WILLIAM A. BARRY, SJ, LETTING GOD COME CLOSE:
AN APPROACH TO THE IGNATIAN SPIRITUAL EXERCISES

Week of Prayer #8:
My Own History of
Sin and Grace

THIS WEEK, WE CONTINUE OUR meditation on sin by considering
how we have chosen sides in the cosmic battle between good and
evil, how we are complicit in the sin of the world, and how we have
experienced the effects of original sin in our lives. Sin is "original"
in that it is a fundamental aspect of the human condition. Yet
grace—God's presence in our lives—is even more "original," or
fundamental, to our existence than sin. Grace always prevails, if
we allow it to.

Try to be very concrete. Note specific actions or patterns of
acting that are sinful, and then go beneath actions or habits to
discern the attitudes, tendencies, and intentions that cause them.
We aim for a graced understanding that cuts to the heart.

Remember that we do this heavy lifting in the context of having experienced ourselves as sinners who are loved. God seeks to
free us from everything that gets in the way of loving ourselves,
others, and God. The focus is not simply naming our sins, which
can itself become a form of self-preoccupation. Instead, we focus
on who God is and who we are before God. With this orientation, we discover the source of our liberation: the boundless mercy
of God. We begin to see how sin has distorted our relationships.
Recognizing how generous and faithful God is, we become dissat-
isfied with our meager, self-directed responses. We naturally want
to reorder our values and make tangible changes. We do this not

out of duty or obligation, but out of love for Someone greater than ourselves.

✝ Prayer for the Week

I pray for the following graces: deepening awareness and sorrow for my sins and a heartfelt experience of God's merciful love for me.

Day 1

> **A Meditation on Our Own Sins** (*SE* 55–61). Ignatius suggests that we use our memory to reflect on our particular history of sin. Notice the specificity of this exercise:
>
> I will call to memory all the sins of my life, looking at them year by year or period by period. For this three things will be helpful: first, the locality or house where I lived; second, the associations which I had with others; third, the occupation I was pursuing. (*SE* 56)

The point here is not to rehearse every sinful moment of your life, which is impossible anyway. Instead, invite God to lead you through your life history and reveal those moments in which you failed to love God, others, or yourself. You may consider specific events or people, or reflect on more general attitudes or patterns of conduct. Ignatius offers the image of making a "court-record of my sins"; you may find another image more helpful.

In your reflection, notice the contagion of sin: how my sin affects my world and others around me. Conclude as Ignatius advises:

Conclude with a **colloquy of mercy**—conversing with God our Lord and thanking him for granting me life until now, and proposing, with his grace, amendment for the future. (*SE* 61)

Day 2

Repetition. In the prayerful consideration of your own sins, keep always in mind God's goodness and mercy. Consider: *God labors through all of creation, through the natural world, through the saints of heaven, and the people in my life to sustain and guide me. So many have loved me and helped me along life's journey. I am filled with wonder at God's generosity—and yet I am ashamed because I still choose to act selfishly or with excessive self-interest. I fail to notice or appreciate the gifts of God (including my talents and abilities). God offers me freedom, yet I choose to be bound by self-preoccupations and petty concerns. I pray, with God's help, to be free of the shackles of sin.*

Conclude with the colloquy of mercy as in Day 1.

Day 3

Read Luke 7:36–50 (Jesus forgives us as he forgives the sinful woman who washes his feet). Place yourself in the scene. Notice how Jesus relates to the woman in her need. Notice the sin of the crowd that surrounds her.

Day 4

Read 2 Samuel 11:1–12:25. Prayerfully read the account of David and his sin. What do you learn about sin and its effects in this age-old story? The Jews have considered David their great king, and Jesus was born into the family line of David. What does this tell us about God's abundant mercy? Are there particular parts of this story that you especially relate to?

Day 5

Read Hosea 11:1–4, 8–9 (God's compassion is like that of a loving parent). Notice your interior responses to the meditations of this week—such as shame, gratitude, peace, sadness, confusion, and hope. What do they say about where your heart is now? What image do you have of God's compassion?

Day 6

As a review of the week, pray the following **triple colloquy** (*SE* 62–63), which Ignatius proposes as a way to demonstrate the sincerity of your sorrow and your desire for conversion in the way you think, feel, and act.

First, pray to Mary, the Mother of God and our Mother.

Pray that Mary ask Jesus Christ, her Son, for the following gifts on your behalf:

- For you to know deep down the rootedness of sin in your life and to truly abhor your sinful tendencies, choices, and actions
- For you to have a deeply felt understanding of how your sins have caused disorder in your life and the world around you
- For you to recognize those things in the world that get in the way of your loving and serving God as you are called
- For you to experience a deep desire to amend your life and turn away from all that is opposed to Christ

Conclude this first colloquy with a Hail Mary.

Second, offer the petitions above to Jesus Christ. Ask him to obtain the same graces for you from God the Father. Conclude with the *Anima Christi* (pp. 41–42).

Third, offer the petitions here directly to God the Father. Conclude with an Our Father.

Notice the beauty of the triple colloquy: even in our very real and visceral struggle with sin, Ignatius reminds us that we are surrounded by divine company and help. We are not alone.

Day 7
Read Psalm 32 ("Happy are those whose transgression is forgiven"). Conclude with the colloquy of mercy from Day 1 of this week or the triple colloquy from Day 6.

For Further Reflection

He who goes about to reform the world must begin with himself, or he loses his labor.

—St. Ignatius of Loyola

Ignatius of Loyola mastered the art of aphorism, reducing timeless truths to a few well-chosen words. These maxims were first collected by a Jesuit scholar in 1712 under the title *Scintillae Ignatianae*. They appear more recently in *Thoughts of St. Ignatius Loyola for Every Day of the Year*, edited by Patrick J. Ryan, SJ.

WEEK OF PRAYER #9:
THE CAUSES AND CONSEQUENCES OF SIN

IN THE COMING TWO WEEKS, we do some repetitions of the previous weeks' exercises. Return to meaningful experiences, not rehashing prayer material but going deeper into significant insights and interior movements. Savor the graces, even if they are difficult ones. Simplify your prayer. Let God's word take root in you.

We strive for greater understanding of

- the influences of the world on our personal choices (we are often not conscious of these influences at first);
- the effect that personal sinful choices have on others and the world;
- the hidden, disordered loves or sinful tendencies that lead us away from love of God, self, and others; and
- the major sins from which other sins flow.

After a lifetime of directing and studying the Exercises, David Fleming, SJ, in his book *What Is Ignatian Spirituality?* distills the nature of sin as follows: "Sin is not the breaking of a law or commandment as much as it is a lack of gratitude. . . . If our heart could truly grasp what God is doing for us, how could we sin? We would be too grateful to sin" (pp. 27–28).

We aim for our understanding of sin to be heartfelt because conversion involves a change in thinking and feeling, in choosing and desiring. With this deepening understanding may come strong affective reactions, including sorrow for sins and gratitude for God's mercy.

This taking stock is not easy, but awareness is a grace when it leads us to freedom *from* a self-centered isolation and freedom *for* loving service of God and others.

✝ Prayer for the Week

I pray for the following graces: growing awareness of the hidden, sinful tendencies that influence my decisions and actions; heartfelt sorrow for my sins; and sincere gratitude for God's mercy and faithfulness to me.

Day 1

Repetition of Luke 7:36–50 (Jesus forgives us as he forgives the sinful woman who washes his feet). Conclude with the colloquy of mercy from Day 1 of week #8 (p. 99).

Day 2

Read Psalm 51 (a psalm of contrition). Conclude with the triple colloquy from Day 6 of week #8 (p. 100).

Day 3

Read Mark 2:13–17 ("I have come to call not the righteous but sinners"). Imagine Jesus calling you as he calls Levi. Conclude with the colloquy before the cross from Day 5 of week #7 (p. 94).

Day 4

Read Matthew 25:31–46 (parable of the last judgment). What do you learn about sin and judgment in this parable? Consider how Jesus portrays sin as a failure to notice and act. Ask: *Whom do I not notice? Am I missing opportunities to love and serve in my life?* Conclude with a colloquy of your choosing.

Day 5

In a final meditation on sin, Ignatius proposes a **meditation on hell** (*SE* 65–72). The point here is not to scare us into conversion, for we have already experienced the tender mercy of God and a desire to amend our lives. The meditation on hell confirms God's mercy and inspires our gratitude. The meditation further reminds us of the ultimate freedom God gives us to embrace or refuse God's love.

In the original text of the *Exercises*, Ignatius, a man of his times, includes many medieval images familiar to us: fire, smoke, sulfur, and tears. David Fleming, SJ offers a contemporary translation of this exercise, which may be more accessible to modern pray-ers:

> St. Paul speaks of our being able to grasp the breadth and length and height and depth of Christ's love and experiencing this love which surpasses all knowledge (Eph 3:18–19). At its opposite pole, I try to experience the breadth and length and height and depth of hell—the despair of facing a cross with no one on it, the turning out upon a world which has no God, the total emptiness of living without purpose, an environment pervasive with hatred and self-seeking, a living death.
>
> I bring the whole of my being into the vividness of this experience. I let all the horror of sin which has been the fruit of my previous prayer periods wash over me in an enveloping flood. In many ways, this setting is the most passive of prayer experiences; it is not a matter of thinking new thoughts or even of looking for new images, but rather entering fully into the felt experience of

sin which has been building up from all my past prayer periods. It is akin to the passive way that my senses take in sights, smells, sounds, tastes, and touches as an automatic datum for my attention. I know that the total felt-environment of sin, in whatever ways it can be most vividly mine, is the setting for this prayer period.

Colloquy: Once I have let the awfulness of this experience sink deep within me, I begin to talk to Christ our Lord about it. I talk to him about all the people who have lived—the many who lived before his coming and who deliberately closed in upon themselves and chose such a hell for all eternity, the many who walked with him in his own country and who rejected his call to love, the many who still keep rejecting the call to love and remain locked in their own chosen hell.

I give thanks to Jesus that he has not allowed me to fall into any of these groups, thus ending my life. All I can do is give thanks to him that up to this moment he has shown himself so loving and merciful to me.

Then I close with an Our Father. (*SE* 66–71)

Day 6

Repetition of the meditation on hell. There are many images of hell in art, literature, and film. We have seen hell on earth in photographs and video images in the news—from Dachau to Darfur, from distant battlefields to our own city streets. We hear the screams of those crushed by systemic poverty and victimized by greed and the lustful pursuit of power. What images of hell speak to you today?

DAY 7

Pray slowly Romans 7:14–25. St. Paul candidly expresses his own inner conflict, which we all can relate to. Note how he ends with thanksgiving. Your weeks should end in the same spirit of thanksgiving.

A Prayer by Karl Rahner, SJ

I should like to speak with you, my God,
and yet what else can I speak of but you?
Indeed, could anything at all exist
which had not been present with you from all eternity,
which didn't have its true home
and most intimate explanation in your mind and heart?
Isn't everything I ever say
really a statement about you?

On the other hand,
if I try, shyly and hesitantly,
to speak to you about yourself,
you will still be hearing about *me*.
For what could I say about you
except that you are *my* God,
The God of my beginning and end,
God of my joy and my need,
God of my life?

KARL RAHNER, SJ (1904–1984), was one of the most influential theologians of the twentieth century. His thought can be discerned in many of the key documents of Vatican II. Rahner believed that theology and spirituality were intimately linked. His books on prayer and the Spiritual Exercises are as compelling as his groundbreaking theological works. For an overview of his life and thought, see "Thursdays with Rahner," by Kevin O'Brien, SJ, in *America*, May 3, 2004, pp. 8–11.

Experiences of Boredom or Dryness in Prayer

OUR RELATIONSHIP WITH GOD IN prayer has a certain rhythm. There are moments of great highs and lows but also very ordinary times. Most of life is in fact quite ordinary. In our prayer life, we can be quick to judge these ordinary times. "Nothing is happening," we may say with frustration, particularly if we feel boredom or dryness when we pray. We can experience a strong temptation to stop praying or to shortchange our prayer time.

When this happens, the first thing to do is resist the temptation. See it for what it is: a temptation to become stingy in your prayer. Remember the generosity with which you began the retreat. Ignatius suggests that we honor the time commitment we made to praying, even staying a few extra minutes when we feel a strong temptation to cut it short (*SE* 12).

Carefully discern feelings of boredom or dryness. Like all interior movements, they can tell you something. Ask yourself:

- **Am I making the necessary preparations for my prayer?** These preparations dispose you to receive the graces God wants to give you. Review the suggestions for praying on pages 23–28 in the introduction of this book.
- **Am I being honest when I pray?** If your prayer is not connected to your real life or your true feelings and thoughts, then boredom and dryness naturally result from this disconnect.

- **Am I working too hard when I pray?** As a general rule, if you feel as if you are working too hard, then you probably are. Such efforts, though well intentioned, indicate that you may be trying to control your prayer too much.

- **Am I being invited to let go of unhelpful images of God or old ways of praying?** Consider trying a new way of praying. Ask a spiritual mentor for help.

- **Am I too attached or addicted to the highs and lows of praying?** Dramatic moments in prayer are very engaging, but they can make ordinary moments of prayer feel like a letdown. Remember, we mostly live in ordinary time. That's just fine because God is found in the ordinary, in the unexciting, regular details of our lives. Consider a significant human relationship in your life. Some of the most meaningful moments occur when nothing exciting is happening but when you are simply enjoying the other's company in the daily routines.

- **Am I letting my own expectations dictate too much of my prayer?** We naturally bring certain desires and expectations to our prayer, as we do to life in general. This is all well and good, but do not let your desires and expectations get in the way of what God wants for you. Expectations may point to your trying to control what happens in prayer. We need to let God take the lead.

Why does God lead us to these ordinary times of praying, which we so quickly label as dry and boring?

- God may be gently tilling the soil of your soul for some future harvest, preparing the ground for a bold insight or a deeper emotional experience to come.

- God may use the times of dryness to heighten your sense of God's presence, so that you will be aware of that presence later in the day or week.

- God may invite you to ordinary times to kindle deep desires and longings. In this case, restlessness is a good thing.

- God may simply want to give you a rest after an intense experience of prayer. Enjoy the stillness and quiet.

Remember, in ordinary times of praying, we may feel that God is not there or not listening. To the contrary, God is there, but not as we imagine or have experienced in the past. Be faithful. God is always close.

Week of Prayer #10:
God's Merciful Love for Me

By this time in the journey, every prayer exercise becomes a repetition of sorts. The mind becomes less and less active with ideas because the subject matter does not change. As a result, the heart is more and more central to the way we respond. Every exercise unfolds the mystery of evil in light of God's continuing protective love. Feel free to return to any of the significant meditations of the past few weeks.

Be real. Abandon any pretense before the God who loves you, who knows you better than you know yourself, and who continues to create in you. God redeems all of your weakness, pain, and sin. God does not take them away: they are a part of your life, but they do not define you. Look forward with hope.

Part of the challenge of these weeks is to truly accept that we are *created*; we are limited beings. We are *not* God, thank God! While striving to become better persons, we let go of the need to be perfect. Slowly and gently God helps us integrate our human limitations in such a way that, while we don't forget them, we can find meaning in them and learn from them. For example, recognizing our own imperfections helps us become more compassionate to others in their weakness.

Journaling will help you distill some of the key lessons of these weeks of heartfelt examination.

Continue the daily practice of the Examen (p. 75–77).

✝ Prayer for the Week

I pray for the following grace: an ever-deepening, heartfelt appreciation of God's merciful love for me.

Day 1

Read 2 Corinthians 12:5–10, with a colloquy ("[The Lord] said to me, 'My grace is sufficient for you, for power is made perfect in weakness.' So, I will boast all the more gladly of my weaknesses, so that the power of Christ may dwell in me"). Can you recall times when you have felt such power, such indwelling of Christ in your life?

Day 2

Read Luke 18:9–14, with a colloquy (parable of the self-righteous Pharisee and the humble tax collector). Can you relate to the Pharisee? The tax collector? Who would you rather be?

Day 3

Read John 8:2–11 (Jesus meets the woman caught in adultery). Imagine this scene. Notice how Jesus looks at the woman. Listen to his words to her and the crowd. Speak to Jesus or the woman as in a colloquy.

Day 4

Repetition of any day.

Day 5

Read Luke 15:1–7, with a colloquy (the Good Shepherd). Do you know what it's like to be lost and then found? Have you acted as a "good shepherd" to another person? As with the parable of the prodigal son and his brother, note how much the Father rejoices when we come home or let ourselves be found. Is there such festivity in your life?

DAY 6

Read Ezekiel 36:25–28, with a colloquy ("A new heart I will give you, and a new spirit I will put within you"). Have you felt what this new heart is for you? Do you see the remains of your "heart of stone"? What new spirit is stirring within you?

DAY 7

Review your journal from the past few weeks. Savor and distill the graces.

For Further Reflection

If you want to make progress in love, speak about love; for holy conversation, like a breeze, fans the flame of charity.

—St. Ignatius of Loyola, in *Thoughts of St. Ignatius Loyola for Every Day of the Year*

Introduction to the Discernment of Spirits

AS WE PRAY THROUGH THE Exercises and rely on the Examen, we become more sensitive to what Ignatius calls the "motions of the soul." These interior movements consist of thoughts, imaginings, emotions, inclinations, desires, feelings, repulsions, and attractions. Recall that during Ignatius's convalescence after his run-in with the cannonball, he noticed different interior movements as he imagined his future. In his autobiography, Ignatius writes (in the third person):

> He did not consider nor did he stop to examine this difference until one day his eyes were partially opened, and he began to wonder at this difference and to reflect upon it. From experience he knew that some thoughts left him sad while others made him happy, and little by little he came to perceive the different spirits that were moving him; one coming from the devil, the other coming from God. (*Autobiography*, no. 8)

In other words, Ignatius believed that these interior movements were the result of "good spirits" and "evil spirits." Spiritual discernment involves reflecting on interior movements to determine where they come from and where they lead us. We try to understand whether a good spirit or evil spirit is acting on us so that we can make good decisions, following the action of a good spirit and rejecting the action of an evil spirit. Discernment of spirits is a means through which we come to understand God's will or desire for us.

Talk of good and evil spirits may seem foreign to modern pray-ers. Psychology gives us other names for what Ignatius called good and evil spirits. We know much more than Ignatius did about human motivations and the influence of culture and groups on an individual psyche. In this book, I continue to use Ignatius's language of good and evil spirits, for it recognizes that evil exists today in many forms. Evil is part of who we are, yet greater than who we are. Haven't we learned in the past few weeks that the cosmic battle between good and evil is waged in the human heart? But remember: just as evil is larger than life, even more so is God's goodness.

In the *Exercises*, Ignatius provides various rules for the discernment of spirits (*SE* 313–36). The following preliminary rules describe how the good spirit and evil spirit generally operate. Their proper application depends on knowing the person in whom the spirits are working.

For people who are caught in a pattern of sin or who have closed themselves off from God's grace, the good spirit shakes them up a bit, making them feel remorseful or unsettled and "stinging their conscience" (*SE* 314). The good spirit tries to get their attention so that they can get back to God. The evil spirit, however, wants nothing more than for such people to continue in their confusion and darkness. So the evil spirit tries to make them complacent, offering excuses and enticing them with further distractions and pleasures.

For people who are growing in faith, hope, and love and trying to live a life pleasing to God, the evil spirit wants to derail them by stirring up anxiety, false sadness, needless confusion, frustration, and other obstacles. In contrast, the good spirit strengthens, encourages, consoles, removes obstacles, and gives peace to such people (*SE* 315). Most people who are praying at this point of the retreat fall in this second category of persons. Thus, be aware of how the evil spirit may get in the way of the retreat; follow the lead of the good spirit who consoles and uplifts you.

In discernment, two terms are used frequently to describe the interior life:

- **Spiritual consolation** is an experience of being so on fire with God's love that we feel impelled to praise, love, and serve God and help others as best as we can. Spiritual consolation encourages and facilitates a deep sense of gratitude for God's faithfulness, mercy, and companionship. In consolation, we feel more alive and connected to others. Ignatius concludes, "Finally, under the word [spiritual] consolation, I include every increase in hope, faith, and charity, and every interior joy which calls and attracts one toward heavenly things and to the salvation of one's soul, by bringing it tranquility and peace in its Creator and Lord" (*SE* 316).

- **Spiritual desolation,** in contrast, is an experience of the soul in heavy darkness or turmoil. We are assaulted by all sorts of doubts. We feel bombarded by temptations and mired in self-preoccupations. We are excessively restless and anxious and feel cut off from others. Such feelings, in Ignatius's words, "move one toward lack of faith and leave one without hope and without love. One is completely listless, tepid, and unhappy, and feels separated from our Creator and Lord" (*SE* 317).

A note of caution: spiritual consolation does not always mean happiness, and spiritual desolation does not always mean sadness. Sometimes an experience of sadness, loneliness, or restlessness is a moment of conversion and intimacy with God and others. Times of human suffering can be moments of grace. For example, accompanying my father as he died was very sad, but I also experienced a profound sense of peace in the intimacy I found with him and my family at that time. Moreover, my remorse over hurting someone can ultimately lead to the joy that comes with reconciliation. In contrast, peace or happiness can be illusory or a form of self-deceit if these feelings are merely covering over issues we need to address. I can feel perfectly happy when I am caught up in a familiar pattern of sin, the effects of which I am blind to. I think, for example, about how easy it is to numb myself with overwork or mindless entertainments or to settle for being content while avoiding a difficult conversation with someone I love. Again the key question is, Where is the movement coming from, and where is it leading me?

Discernment requires affective maturity, inner quiet, and an ability to attend to one's interior life. Discernment takes practice, and we learn to "discern the spirits" by trial and error. The Examen is the daily practice of discernment and should be incorporated regularly in your retreat. Discernment is also an art. Ignatius provides wise and specific rules for discernment, but often we have to improvise and adjust because God works in each of us so uniquely. A wise spiritual guide or companion can help you sift through strong interior movements.

In the upcoming weeks, we will discuss more of Ignatius's rules for the discernment of spirits. As much as you can, try to apply these rules to your retreat in daily life. In all you do, strive to follow the lead of God working through "good spirits," your own good judgment, and good people in your life.

> In the case of those who are going from good to better, the good angel touches the soul gently, lightly, and sweetly, like a drop of water going into a sponge. The evil spirit touches it sharply, with noise and disturbance, like a drop of water falling onto a stone (*SE* 335).

The "Second Week"

†

Accompanying Jesus Christ on Mission

AFTER THREE YEARS OF PHILOSOPHY and theology studies at Fordham, I was sent to St. Joseph's University in Philadelphia to teach introductory philosophy and ethics. This stage of a Jesuit's formation is much anticipated. Five years after entering the novitiate, the Jesuit gets to work full-time in ministry for a couple of years before returning for more theology studies in preparation for ordination. This type of assignment is why we become Jesuits in the first place: to "help souls" as Ignatius often wrote, or in today's terms, to help people and serve the greatest needs of the church and the world that are not being met.

After my first year teaching at St. Joseph's, I asked to spend the summer working with the Jesuit Refugee Service, an organization founded in 1980 to respond to the refugee crises of that time. The problem, as we know, has only gotten worse as the number of refugees and internally displaced persons continues to grow with widespread wars, civil unrest, famine, economic catastrophe, and natural disaster. In my studies and my teaching, I explored from many angles and sources the concept of human dignity, long enshrined in Catholic social thought. With JRS, I wanted to see how that concept is made concrete in the promotion of human rights for refugees and other displaced persons.

In the United States JRS spends considerable resources advocating on behalf of refugees and migrants before national and international governmental bodies. It also staffs chaplaincy programs that provide pastoral care and religious services for non-citizens detained by Immigration and Customs Enforcement in various detention facilities across the country. While collaborating with organizations that provide legal assistance and humanitarian aid, JRS views its primary role as accompanying the noncitizen amid the ups and downs of life in a detention facility or refugee camp: being present to them in their confinement, "walking" alongside them as best we can. Ideally, a relationship of solidarity develops, wherein the JRS worker also learns from the refugees something about faith and values. Such befriending and learning on the ground helps JRS advocate for refugees more effectively in places of power. This faithful accompaniment invites others to consider the world and the world's problems from the perspective of people who live on the margins.

People placed in detention live a provisional existence. They await the outcome of asylum or deportation hearings. The process can take weeks, months, or years, and deportations can occur at any time. I was sent to one of the several detention centers in Southern California, San Pedro (now closed), located at Los Angeles Harbor. I was covering for Peter, a dynamic Jesuit chaplain, who was going to take some well-deserved time off. Peter showed me around the cramped facility, which was basically a jail: five floors divided into sections (or "pods"), common rooms for meals and recreation (which basically meant playing cards and watching television), a small medical clinic, a library with scant offerings, and a couple of concrete yards for outdoor recreation (lifting weights, basketball, and walking laps). From the yards you could hear the tantalizing sounds of the ocean, see the cruise ships leaving the harbor, and smell the salty breezes.

After a couple of days of introductions, off Peter went on vacation, and there I stood, on very unfamiliar territory. After six years of itinerant Jesuit life, however, I had learned to adapt and throw myself into new situations, despite feeling absolutely petrified deep inside.

Miguel became one of my first mentors. This twentysomething had been in San Pedro for six months. He helped me negotiate the various personalities among the men. His English was much better than my Spanish: he told me who needed help and who would not appreciate a chaplain's call that day. His story was typical of so many there. Miguel had lived in the United States most of his life, having immigrated from Mexico with his parents, and without papers, when he was a boy. He had somehow gotten on the radar screen of the immigration authorities: usually a workplace audit, a traffic stop, or a criminal offence attracts attention. Miguel now faced leaving all his family in the United States and returning to Mexico, the country of his birth but little else. Knowing that deportation was likely, he was already planning how to get back to his family in the United States.

He introduced me to Luis, a quiet man in his fifties who spent most of his days drawing inside the rec room. We often prayed together. I struggled to offer some words of solace from the Bible in my barely proficient Spanish. After a few weeks, Luis gave me a sketch of the Virgin of Guadalupe, which I have framed and that hangs prominently in my office today. For Mexicans in particular, the Virgin Mary, a friend of the poor, is a powerful intercessor and protector amid the loneliness and anxiety of detention.

Each week I joined one of the women's pods for Mass, celebrated by Rob, the Jesuit director of the local JRS office. As there was no chapel, our altar was one of the steel tables in the corner of the rec room. The inane chatter of morning talk shows blared from the other end of the room. For the ten or fifteen women who came to Mass each week, our corner was a sanctuary. We sang more loudly than the television, and the prayers were from the heart. The petitions took a long time, as each woman usually prayed for someone at length.

Most typically, they prayed for children left behind in the United States. Ana had been cleaning hotel rooms in Palm Springs for nearly a decade. Her undocumented status was revealed when the immigration authorities audited the books of the hotel where she worked. She had left her two children, born in the United States, with her sister. Her husband was in another detention center. Every day in tears, she asked me to pray that she may be reunited with her children, who visited her on Sundays, taking several buses to see her. Another woman refused to let her children come to San Pedro: she did not want them to see her dressed like a criminal in her blue jumpsuit.

In the basement of San Pedro, there were some isolation cells for people needing to be separated from the general population: those prone to fighting; those threatened by rival gangs; those suffering from AIDS; and those targeted for harassment because they were gay, lesbian, or transgendered. These visits I found the most heart wrenching. Isolation, even for a short time, can do terrible things to the mind and soul. Worst of all, in the relative darkness and with limited human contact, the person begins to lose hope. Thus, when I came, they were eager to see me. I had to meet with them through a small opening in the cell door. Down there, I did not have to say much, because they talked, usually too quickly for me to follow their Spanish. My responses were very simple: *Dios te ama; tú no estás solo: el Señor está contigo; ten esperanza* (God loves you; you are not alone: the Lord is with you; have hope). I discovered that sometimes the best counsel is the simplest.

Each day, I did my best to walk alongside those in detention at San Pedro. I tried to be of comfort to them, a faithful presence in their otherwise transient and unpredictable lives. From them, I learned much about the resilience of faith in dire circumstances. When all else was lost, so many threw themselves on the Lord for consolation and hope. They also leaned on one another. I was deeply consoled seeing how they looked after one another, becoming like family in their shared grief. I came to learn that all of us, no matter what government papers we have, share a very human longing to be with those we love, to settle down and to make a home, and to find a place on earth to call our own. I also witnessed how powerful hope can be and how people who hope live differently; this was a theme of Pope Benedict's encyclical on hope, referenced repeatedly on his visit to the United States in 2008.

In the **Second Week** of the Spiritual Exercises, Ignatius invites us to accompany Jesus Christ from his birth through his public ministry. In the First Week, our gaze was much on ourselves; now God lifts our gaze and turns our attention to Jesus as he walked and talked, healed and preached, among us. The grace of the Second Week is fundamental: to grow in a heartfelt knowledge of Jesus Christ so that we can love him more deeply and follow him more closely. But to grow in this intimate love, we need to get close. We need to walk with God, who became one with us.

In this part of the adventure, the Gospels come alive for us. We are there with Jesus, immersed in the Gospels with the help of our senses and imagination. We do not simply obtain more insight or information. With our attentiveness fine-tuned and our imaginations sparked, we see the living God in daily life as we pray through the Exercises. For example, Ignatius invites the retreatant to pray over Matthew's account of Joseph, Mary, and the newborn baby Jesus fleeing to Egypt to escape the murderous wrath of Herod in Bethlehem (Matthew 2:13–23). In today's stories of refugees and displaced persons who make their own tragic journey of tears, we meet Joseph, Mary, and Jesus on the run.

One of the last images I have of my work with JRS is that of the Holy Family. On Wednesdays, I visited a minimum security juvenile detention facility that included a mix of young people at risk: U.S. citizens who committed a crime, noncitizens who were picked up by immigration authorities, and runaways from all over the U.S. The undocumented minors were housed with the runaways in one cinder block dormitory in a corner of the large campus. Ten girls bunked on one side of the dorm, and the boys stayed on the other, joined by a small common room. They could move about freely but remained under the constant and watchful gaze of a supervisor.

Luke was a sixteen-year-old who ran away from an abusive parent in Texas and was found living on the beaches of southern California. (Drug dealing or prostitution was not part of his story, as is common for teenage runaways). He seemed older than his years, toughened by his hard youth. He could lash out in anger at times, but I could detect an undercurrent of gentleness and boyish idealism. Luke was among the oldest in the group. María had come from El Salvador to reach one of her parents, who lived in the United States. She had been picked up crossing the border in the desert with a group of relatives from her village. María's beautiful face and eyes revealed both a youthful shyness and a very adult confidence. In Spanish, she told me that she felt alone and scared, but she never showed it to the others. About Luke's age, María liked to mother the younger girls she bunked with.

Amazingly, this motley group of native-born American runaways and undocumented Latin Americans got along despite the language barriers and different histories, not to mention the pressures that came with life on the run. They bonded over card games in the common room and basketball games on the court near their dorm. They had no one else but each other.

On my last Wednesday visit, before heading back east for the start of the academic year, I pulled Luke and María aside to tell them I was leaving. I told them, "Now I leave you in charge, to look after everyone, especially the littlest. Take care of them when they are sad or lonely."

"Don't worry, Father," Luke said. (I wore a collar on my visits, so they assumed I was ordained, which was still some years away.) "We'll take care of them," he assured me. María smiled knowingly and with pride. An hour later, as I left, I turned and saw them. María had on her lap a small girl who was crying, and Luke was rounding up the stragglers who were late for dinner in the common room. They all sat down together for their family meal, a Holy Family.

A Prayer for Óscar Romero
and Other Departed Priests

It helps, now and then, to step back and take a long view.
The kingdom is not only beyond our efforts,
it is even beyond our vision.

We accomplish in our lifetime only a tiny fraction
of the magnificent enterprise that is God's work.

Nothing we do is complete, which is a way of saying
that the kingdom always lies beyond us.

No statement says all that could be said.
No prayer fully expresses our faith.
No confession brings perfection.
No pastoral visit brings wholeness.
No program accomplishes the church's mission.
No set of goals and objectives includes everything.

It may be incomplete,
but it is a beginning, a step along the way,
an opportunity for the Lord's grace to enter and do the rest.
We may never see the end results, but that is the difference
between the master builder and the worker.
We are workers, not master builders; ministers not messiahs.
We are prophets of a future not our own.

This is what we are about.
We plant the seeds that one day will grow.
We water seeds already planted,
knowing that they hold future promise.
We lay foundations that will need further development.

We provide yeast that produces far beyond our capabilities.
We cannot do everything, and there is a sense of liberation
in realizing that. This enables us to do something,
and to do it very well.
Amen.

ÓSCAR ROMERO (1917–1980) was archbishop of San Salvador. A zealous advocate for the poor of his country and a tireless voice for reconciliation amid civil war, Romero was assassinated while saying Mass. Though widely attributed to Romero, the prayer was actually offered by Cardinal John Dearden of Detroit in a homily in 1979. Dearden was a kindred spirit to Romero: both preached peace and justice as central to the gospel.

Week of Prayer #11:
The Contemplation
on the Incarnation

WE NOW MOVE TO THE next phase of Ignatius's Exercises: the
Second Week. In the First Week, we savored the grace of being
loved by God in our sinfulness. In the Second Week, we naturally
respond to God's mercy by wanting to get to know this God who
is so generous and loving, who calls us by name, just as we are.

In *Letting God Come Close*, an insightful overview of the
movements of the Exercises, William Barry, SJ describes the shift
in orientation as follows: in the First Week, "the focus has been
on us and our needs. We wanted to know in a heartfelt way that
God is where we are, with us in our brokenness, our sinfulness,
our desperate need." In the Second Week, however, "we now want
to be where Jesus is; we want to know him and his values and his
mission, and we want to be part of that mission" (p. 78).

In the Second Week, we accompany Jesus in his earthly ministry. We seek not scientific or biographical facts about Jesus, but a
knowledge more akin to knowing a friend in mystery and depth—
a heartfelt knowledge.

Before we dwell on the story of Jesus' life, Ignatius invites us to
look at the big picture. In the Contemplation on the Incarnation,
we gaze on the world with the Trinity—with God who is Father,
Son, and Holy Spirit. We get lost in the mystery of the Incarnation.
We marvel at how God works through ordinary people like Mary
and Joseph. We are filled with great gratitude because God wanted

to get close to us by becoming human in Jesus of Nazareth. In this way, God makes divine love imminently available to all people.

✝ Prayer for the Week

I pray for the following graces: a deeply felt knowledge of God's dream for the world; awe and wonder at the mystery of the Incarnation.

Day 1

Contemplation on the Incarnation (*SE* 101–9). In the Exercises, a contemplation refers to imaginative prayer. Ignatius was convinced, through his own experience, that God speaks to us in our imaginings. Here, we begin the contemplation by imagining the three Divine Persons gazing on "the whole surface or circuit of the world, full of people" (*SE* 102).

With this perspective, consider what the Divine Persons (and you) see and hear: men and women of different sizes, shapes, and colors; rich and poor; old and young. People speaking different languages. Some being born, others dying; some running and playing, others sick and suffering. Some laughing, others crying. Some screaming and shouting, others praying and singing.

With the gaze of the Trinity, consider how people are treating one another: some loving, others hating; some hugging, others hitting; some helping, others ignoring, hurting, and killing. What do you see and hear?

How do you feel as you imagine the world in this way? How do the three Divine Persons respond to the joys and sufferings of the world? How does the God who is Love respond to us, God's children, who are lost, aimless, suffering, sinning, confused, and hurting?

Hear the Divine Persons saying, "Let us work the redemption of the human race" (*SE* 107).

What words do you want to speak to God, who is Father, Son, and Holy Spirit?

Day 2

Repetition. God saves us in the details of our lives, in the beauty and brokenness of our world. Continue to gaze upon the world today with the perspective of the Trinity. You might consider your own particular community and living situation.

What do the Divine Persons (and you) see and hear? How does your heart respond? How does God labor to save the world today in very concrete ways?

If you like, pray with John 1:1–5, 14–18 ("the Word became flesh").

Day 3

Read Luke 1:26–38 (the Annunciation). God responds to the "groaning" of creation very concretely. Narrow your imaginative gaze from a broad perspective and focus on the details of how God saves in history: "See in particular the house and rooms of Mary, in the city of Nazareth in the province of Galilee" (*SE* 103). Imagine the sights, sounds, and smells of the scene, when the angel Gabriel greets the young woman. Listen to their conversation. Notice the expressions on their faces and the movement of their bodies. Conclude by praying a colloquy with Mary.

Day 4

Repetition of the Annunciation. In his contemporary translation of the *Exercises*, David Fleming suggests the following for our consideration of this scene: "Notice how our triune God works—so simply and quietly, so patiently. A world goes on, apparently oblivious to the new creation which has begun. I take in Mary's complete way of being available and responding to her Lord and God" (p. 93).

Day 5

Read Luke 1:39–56 (Mary visits Elizabeth). Again, use your imagination to pray with this scene. Notice how God saves within a particular family. Marvel at how God needs the help of these gracious women to "work the redemption of the human race" (*SE* 107) Pray Mary's Magnificat with her, in a spirit of joy.

Day 6

Read Matthew 1:18–25 (Joseph's dream). God again relies on human freedom and cooperation to save us in our need. Be with Joseph as he generously and courageously responds to God's calling him to become a husband and father. Hear how the angel comforts Joseph, telling him not to be afraid, just as the angel Gabriel urged Mary. Love dispels all fear.

Day 7

Savor the graces of the week, or make a repetition of one of the previous Scripture passages.

Undertake nothing without consulting God.

—St. Ignatius of Loyola, in *Thoughts of St. Ignatius Loyola for Every Day of the Year*

For Further Reflection

Consider a blissfully happy couple finding all they need in one another. For no other reason than generosity and the desire to share their happiness, they decide to adopt children as their own. From then on their life undergoes a profound change. Now they are vulnerable; their happiness is wrapped up in the welfare of the children; things can never be the same again.

If the children choose to alienate themselves and start on the path to ruin, the couple are stricken. They will plead, humble themselves, make huge sacrifices, go out of themselves to get their loved ones to understand that the home is still their home, that the love they have been given is unchanging.

This perhaps, gives us some insight into redemption. In a mystery we cannot fathom, God "empties," "loses" Himself, in bringing back to Himself His estranged, lost children. And this is all the Father wants. This is the only remedy for His wound. God is no longer pure God, but always God-with-humanity-in-His-heart.

—RUTH BURROWS, *ESSENCE OF PRAYER*

Ruth Burrows, a Carmelite nun who has written extensively about the spiritual life, offers this analogy to help us understand what incarnation and redemption mean for us: *why does God become one of us?*

Gentle Reminders

AT THIS POINT IN THE retreat, pray-ers have likely developed a habit or certain style of praying. We naturally fall into a rhythm that will carry us forward on the wings of grace. Sometimes, however, we can become sloppy after being in the retreat for many weeks. Structure is important to the Exercises. Although we cannot force God's hand or make grace happen, we can dispose ourselves to grace by following Ignatius's spiritual framework.

As you continue praying, recall the suggestions for prayer offered at the beginning of this book on pages 23–28:

Before Your Prayer

Review the prayer material before your prayer period (such as the night before).

Maintain an environment conducive to prayer, free of distractions. Pay attention to your breathing and posture.

Offer your time of prayer to God. Pray to be open to the working of the Spirit. Use whatever words, images, or rituals are natural for you to compose yourself.

During Your Prayer

Pray for the grace you desire, either as suggested in the prayer materials or in your own words. What do you want God to do for you? How do you want God to be present to you?

As you use the prayer materials, remember that they are not homework or tasks to check off a list. Be flexible and adapt the retreat to where you are.

Do not run ahead of the grace. Be patient; don't rush to finish the weeks of the retreat. Follow the lead of the Spirit, not a timetable.

If you feel like you are working too hard, you probably are. Avoid trying to problem solve or to be "productive" in your prayer.

Avoid comparisons with how others pray or progress through the retreat.

Include a colloquy in every prayer period: the more natural and conversational it is, the better.

Conclude your prayer with an Our Father, Hail Mary, *Anima Christi*, or another favorite prayer.

Pray for thirty to forty-five minutes a day. Do not significantly increase or decrease this sacred time.

After Your Prayer

Reflect on your time of prayer; if possible, do this in a place different from where you prayed.

Pay attention to consolations, desolations, and other significant interior movements. In your journal, note these movements, along with important images, words, memories, or moods. Note any connections from your prayer to your daily life.

Pray the Examen (pp. 75–77) at some other point in your day. This prayer is key to developing a habit of discernment.

Maintain the spirit of generosity with which you began the retreat:

> The persons who make the Exercises will benefit greatly by entering upon them with great spirit and generosity toward their Creator and Lord, and by offering all their desires and freedom to him so that His Divine Majesty can make use of their persons and of all they possess in whatsoever way is in accord with his most holy will. (*SE* 5)

WEEK OF PRAYER #12: THE BIRTH OF JESUS

HAVING REJOICED WITH MARY IN her "yes" to God, we begin to walk with Jesus from his birth, through his hidden life and public ministry, to the foot of the cross at Calvary. In these weeks, we ask repeatedly for a grace fundamental to the Second Week of the Exercises: to know Jesus *more* intimately, to love him *more* intensely, and to follow him *more* closely (*SE* 104). This idea of the "more"—encapsulated in the Latin word, *magis*—is vital for Ignatius. The Exercises are intended to tap into a zeal that impels us to more knowledge, love, and service of God and others.

The order of these graces is important. We can rush to find out what our calling in life is, without really knowing the One who calls us. If we focus on first knowing and loving Jesus, then the call to serve becomes clearer and we can approach it with less fear. We really cannot love someone unless we first know him or her on some deeply personal level. Ultimately, it is possible to follow Jesus, with the sacrifice that entails, only if we are rooted in our love for him.

As with our contemplation on the Incarnation, we will rely on imaginative prayer in these weeks. (For more on this Ignatian way of praying, see the chapter that follows.) In praying with Scripture, we want to pay attention to concrete details because God works for our redemption in the particular beauty and brokenness of our world.

✝ Prayer for the Week

I pray for the following grace: to know Jesus more intimately, to love him more intensely, and to follow him more closely.

Day 1

Contemplation on the Nativity (*SE* 110–17). Pray the familiar story of Luke 2:1–7. Ignatius suggests imagining the details of the scene:

> Recall how Our Lady, pregnant almost nine months and, as we may piously meditate, seated on an ass, together with Joseph and a servant girl leading an ox, set forth from Nazareth to go to Bethlehem and pay the tribute which Caesar has imposed on all those lands. (*SE* 111)

> [Imagine] the place. Here it will be to see in imagination the road from Nazareth to Bethlehem. Consider its length and breadth, whether it is level or winds through valleys and hills. Similarly, look at the place or cave of the Nativity: How big is it, or small? How low or high? And how is it furnished? (*SE* 112)

> Behold and consider what they are doing; for example, journeying and toiling, in order that the Lord may be born in greatest poverty; and that after so many hardships of hunger, thirst, heat, cold, injuries, and insults, he may die on the cross! And all this for me! (*SE* 116)

In imagining the other details of the birth of Jesus, Ignatius suggests placing yourself directly in the scene:

> See the persons; that is, to see Our Lady, Joseph,
> the maidservant, and the infant Jesus after
> his birth. I will make myself a poor, little, and
> unworthy slave, gazing at them, contemplating
> them, and serving them in their needs, just as if
> I were there, with all possible respect and rever-
> ence. (*SE* 114)

Conclude as usual with a colloquy with Mary or Joseph, or
with God the Father, or even by speaking to the baby Jesus
while holding him. Or perhaps you may want to just sit in the
peaceful silence of the night.

Day 2
Repetition.

Day 3
Read Luke 2:8–20. Continue contemplating the Nativity. Join
the shepherds in the countryside and then journey with them
to visit the baby Jesus. As you pray through Jesus' life, you
will notice how often he surrounds himself with people like
the shepherds—those who are poor and on the margins of
society. Rejoicing in the good news of Jesus' birth, the shepherds become Jesus' first disciples.

Day 4
Read Matthew 2:1–12. Accompany the wise men on the journey to Jesus.

Day 5
Repetition of one of the scenes of the Nativity. See also Isaiah
52:7–10 ("All the ends of the earth shall see the salvation of
our God").

Day 6

A different kind of repetition—**application of the five senses** (*SE* 121–26). In our contemplations thus far, we have been imagining the Gospel scenes, immersing ourselves in the details of Jesus' life. Here, Ignatius invites us to deepen our prayer. We become less active: we are more about being than doing. We do less thinking than in our meditations and less imagining than in our contemplations. We become more still, savoring the graces and resting in the presence of God. You may quietly review with Jesus your prayer over several days, or rest in one particular scene or conversation that meant something to you in your prayer.

We let go. We let the story of Jesus become a part of us. In the same way that our bodily senses take in the data of daily life, we let the sights, sounds, smells, tastes, and feelings of our contemplations wash over us, and we allow whatever insights, images, desires, or emotions that remain to take root in us.

Day 7

Savor the graces of the week.

Ignatian Contemplation: Imaginative Prayer

IGNATIUS WAS CONVINCED THAT GOD can speak to us as surely through our imagination as through our thoughts and memories. In the Ignatian tradition, praying with the imagination is called contemplation. In the Exercises, contemplation is a very active way of praying that engages the mind and heart and stirs up thoughts and emotions. (Note that in other spiritual traditions, *contemplation* has quite a different meaning: it refers to a way of praying that frees the mind of all thoughts and images).

Ignatian contemplation is suited especially for the Gospels. In the Second Week of the Exercises, we accompany Jesus through his life by imagining scenes from the Gospel stories. Let the events of Jesus' life be present to you right now. Visualize the event as if you were making a movie. Pay attention to the details: sights, sounds, tastes, smells, and feelings of the event. Lose yourself in the story; don't worry if your imagination is running too wild. At some point, place yourself in the scene.

Contemplating a Gospel scene is not simply remembering it or going back in time. Through the act of contemplation, the Holy Spirit makes present a mystery of Jesus' life in a way that is meaningful for you now. Use your imagination to dig deeper into the story so that God may communicate with you in a personal, evocative way.

We might initially worry about going beyond the text of the Gospel. If you have offered your time of prayer to God, then begin by trusting that God is communicating with you. If you wonder if your imagination is going "too far," then do some discernment with how you are praying. Where did your imagining lead you: Closer to God or farther away? Is your imagining bringing you consolation or desolation?

Some people find imaginative prayer difficult. They may not be able to picture the scene easily, yet they may have some intuition or gut reaction to the story. Or they may hear or feel the story more than visualize it. In a spirit of generosity, pray as you are able; don't try to force it. Rest assured that God will speak to you, whether through your memory, understanding, intellect, emotions, or imagination.

Week of Prayer #13: The Childhood of Jesus

WE CONTINUE TO CONTEMPLATE THE early life of Jesus. We notice how Jesus grows up in a particular social, economic, political, and religious context. Even in the comforting stories of the Nativity, we see the beginnings of opposition against Jesus. We cannot separate the saving work of Christ from the times in which he lived. Salvation does not take place apart from the world, as if God were throwing a lifeline down from heaven and pulling us up. Instead, God saves *in* the world.

God continues to save us in the details of our lives today, in the beauty and messiness of our world. As we pray in the midst of daily life, we may become more sensitive to the joys and tragedies of our world and to the needs of people around us. In accompanying the Holy Family in their flight to Egypt and their return to Nazareth, how can we not feel deeply the plight of millions of displaced persons in our world? How can we not be more attentive to the supports and the pressures that young families experience today?

Contemplate the Gospel scenes, as before, with your imagination. Become a part of the scene as if you were there. Enter a conversation with those present, as in a colloquy. Notice how Mary and Joseph teach Jesus how to love and how to be fully human.

In the Gospel contemplations, Ignatius often instructs us to pray "so as to draw some profit." This does not mean that we have to be "productive" when we pray, analyzing the text to find some insightful application. The review of prayer (journaling) is a better time to use the intellect to draw real-world applications.

In contemplation, we let our prayer affect us and touch our hearts. We allow memories, emotions, desires, and longings to be stirred as God wishes.

✝ Prayer for the Week

I pray for the following grace: to know Jesus more intimately, to love him more intensely, and to follow him more closely.

Day 1
Read Luke 2:21–38. Accompany the Holy Family as Jesus is named and then presented in the temple. Join Simeon and Anna as they wait for Jesus and then as they meet him.

Day 2
Repetition.

Day 3
Read Isaiah 9:1–7. As you marvel at the child Jesus, what hopes spring in your heart? What names do you give the child?

Day 4
Read Matthew 2:13–23. Accompany Joseph, Mary, and Jesus as they escape into exile. Spend time with them in Egypt, and join them on their return to Nazareth.

Day 5
Repetition.

Day 6
Application of the five senses (p. 140).

Day 7
Savor the graces of the week.

Rules for Discernment of Spirits: How the Good Spirit and Evil Spirit Operate

AT THIS POINT OF THE retreat, the good spirit and the evil spirit work in typical ways. God wants us to continue growing in faith, hope, and love. God desires that we come to know and love the Son more intimately. God kindles in us great hopes and a zeal to serve God and others.

Conversely, the evil spirit, which Ignatius also calls the "enemy of our human nature," wants to discourage us and get us off course. Sometimes the evil spirit's tactics are obvious: causing extreme doubt, confusion, anxiety, and temptation. As we grow in the spiritual life, the enemy must adjust its tactics and become more subtle, even using experiences of spiritual consolation for evil ends or suggesting thoughts that seem good and holy but actually lead us away from the praise, love, and service of God.

> It is characteristic of God and his angels, by the motions they cause, to give genuine happiness and spiritual joy, and thereby to banish any sadness and turmoil induced by the enemy. It is characteristic of the enemy to fight against this happiness and spiritual consolation, by using specious reasonings, subtleties, and persistent deceits. (*SE* 329)

> In the case of those who are going from good
> to better, the good angel touches the soul gently,
> lightly, and sweetly, like a drop of water going
> into a sponge. The evil spirit touches it sharply,
> with noise and disturbance, like a drop of water
> falling onto a stone. (*SE* 335)

In our prayer, we become more aware of significant movements of the soul (such as thoughts, feelings, desires, and intuitions). We begin to understand whether a movement comes from the good spirit or evil spirit by noticing where a movement leads us. With experience, we learn to follow the lead of the good spirit and, conversely, to resist acting on the movement of the evil spirit.

Consider one significant interior movement that you experienced this week. Was it the action of the good spirit or evil spirit?

Week of Prayer #14: The Hidden Life of Jesus

THIS WEEK, WE CONTEMPLATE THE "hidden life" of Jesus, those years of his boyhood and young adulthood in Nazareth mentioned only briefly in the Gospels. Given the scant reference in Scripture, you will supply many of the details through imaginative prayer. We ask the Spirit to show us what Jesus was like growing up. Accompany him as a friend, relative, or neighbor in Nazareth. Though fully divine, Jesus is also fully human (like us in all things but sin, our tradition teaches). Notice, then, how Jesus grows into his humanity.

It doesn't matter whether or not the details you supply are historically accurate. We are not reconstructing history. Instead, with the inspiration of the Holy Spirit, we are coming to know Jesus more intimately so that we can love him more dearly and follow him more closely.

When contemplating the Gospels, we are often gifted with memories from our lives that correspond in some way to Jesus' life. These memories can be gifts because through our prayerful remembering, past hurts may be healed. Or we may appreciate how God has been at work in unexpected or previously overlooked ways. Or we may gain some insight into significant events in our history. Some memories may be painful, of course, so we must be gentle with our remembering and seek help from others when needed.

✝ Prayer for the Week

I pray for the following grace: to know Jesus more intimately, to love him more intensely, and to follow him more closely.

Day 1
Read Luke 2:39–40. Contemplate Jesus' boyhood and growing up until the age of twelve.

Day 2
Read Luke 2:41–50. Accompany Jesus on his journey to the temple, where he experiences a deepening sense of his vocation. Be present to Mary and Joseph in their concern. Share with them the experiences of your own youth and how you feel about them now, looking back.

Day 3
Read Luke 2:51–52. Live with Jesus during some portions of his teenage years and young adulthood. Remember that at some point during Jesus' youth, Joseph, his father, died. Share with Jesus experiences of your own youth and coming of age.

Day 4
Repetition.

Day 5
Repetition. Or pray Psalm 42 with the young Jesus. Remember that Jesus, a faithful Jew, would have prayed these psalms as a young man in his own language. The psalms helped him express his faith in God the Father; they can help us in the same way

Day 6
Read Matthew 3:13. Spend time with Jesus as he prepares to leave home and makes his way to the Jordan River to begin his

public ministry. What do Mary and Jesus say to each other? What stories do they share about Jesus' growing up?

Day 7
Savor the graces of the week.

Rules for Discernment of Spirits: Storing Up the Graces of Consolation

IN THE SPIRITUAL LIFE, WE naturally have moments of both consolation and desolation. We need to discern which is present because we deal with them differently. In times of consolation and desolation, Ignatius offers practical advice:

> One who is in consolation should consider how he or she will act in future desolation, and store up new strength for that time. (*SE* 323)

> In contrast, one who is in desolation should reflect that with the sufficient grace already available he or she can do much to resist all hostile forces, by drawing strength from our Creator and Lord. (*SE* 324)

In other words, store up consolations so that when desolation comes, you are less likely to become mired in doubt, confusion, or discouragement. You will remember that God is faithful and has not left you alone. In the absence of the good feelings that often accompany consolation, choose to think about and remember the consolation of the past and anticipate with hope the consolation that is surely to come again, if you are open to it.

Consolation is a gift. Thus, Ignatius advises in the Rules, "One who is in consolation ought to be humble" (*SE* 324). Grace is God's doing, not ours. We cannot force grace or fake it. So in times of consolation, we thank God for the gift of God's presence and encouragement.

WEEK OF PRAYER #15: THE CALL OF CHRIST, OUR KING

WE PRAY WITH ANOTHER KEY exercise in Ignatius's school of prayer: the Call of Christ, our King. The kingdom (or reign) of God is a central symbol in the biblical tradition. Like any symbol, the kingdom of God has many layers of meaning. Most basically, it expresses God's dream for the world. Imagine what the world would look like if everyone acknowledged God as Creator and Lord and if everyone followed God's law of love and life! Jesus spoke of the kingdom of God and revealed most completely God's dream of the world in how he lived, taught, healed, and served others.

Note the grace we ask for this week: we ask not to be deaf to Christ's call in our life and to be willing to do what Christ asks of us (*SE* 91). Praying through this exercise, we recall our colloquy before the cross during the First Week, when we asked, "What ought I do for Christ?" Christ calls us out of great love and concern for us and our world; ideally, we respond also in love and not in fear or obligation.

At times, we may resist opening our ears to Christ's call because we are afraid of what we'll hear (for example, we may not want to change something about our lifestyle). Or we may resist because we have an image of God as imposing the divine will on us to make us pay for some past sin. To the contrary, God's call is meant to give us a fuller life of deeper meaning and authentic joy (though not without the sacrifices that accompany a life of discipleship). Far from being imposed from above, God's will—or God's desire—for us is found in our own deepest, truest desires.

Such honesty about our fears and resistances is helpful. If you cannot honestly ask for the grace of this week, then Ignatius would suggest that you pray for the desire to ask for the grace. Be honest.

At this point in the Exercises, we don't have to make any offering or commitment if we're not ready. For now, we just want to be open enough to hear the call and to get excited about Christ's engaging vision for us and the world. We want to taste the disciples' zeal for mission. We allow God's Spirit to inspire holy desires. We let God work on us.

✝ Prayer for the Week

I pray for the following graces: to listen more attentively to Christ's call in my life; to become more ready and eager to do what Christ wants.

Day 1
Contemplation of the Kingdom of Jesus Christ (*SE* 91–98). This contemplation has two parts. We begin by contemplating the call of a worldly leader, which then leads us to consider the call of Christ, our King. In considering the call of a worldly leader, Ignatius relies on language and feudal images fitting for his time and for his own history as a knight-in-training:

> First, I will place before my mind a human king, chosen by God our Lord himself, whom all Christian princes and all Christian persons reverence and obey. (*SE* 92)

> Second, I will observe how this king speaks to all his people, saying, "My will is to conquer the whole land of the infidels. Hence, whoever wishes to come with me has to be content

with the same food I eat, and the drink, and the clothing which I wear, and so forth. So too each one must labor with me during the day, and keep watch in the night, and so on, so that later each may have a part with me in the victory, just as each has shared in the toil." (*SE* 93)

Third, I will consider what good subjects ought to respond to a king so generous and kind; and how, consequently, if someone did not answer his call, he would be scorned and upbraided by everyone and accounted as an unworthy knight. (*SE* 94)

If the medieval imagery is distracting or unhelpful, consider the inspiration of a person of our time who personifies virtue and integrity, fights against injustice, or labors for the oppressed and marginalized. This person may be a civic leader, a modern-day saint or prophet, or a personal friend. Or you may rely on some mythical figure in literature or film. Reflect on anyone who inspires you and summons your zeal to make the world a more just and gentle place.

Day 2
Contemplation of the Kingdom of Jesus Christ, continued. We now consider the call of Jesus Christ. Note the repeated use of two phrases, the "more" (or "greater") and "with me." Christ summons the best from us, calling us to the *magis*, to greater service and generosity. While we rightly avoid perfectionism and workaholism, we strive for excellence in our laboring for the kingdom. Mediocrity has no place in the disciple's response: the stakes are too high, and God is just too good to deserve a meager response from us. Moreover, the invitation is to labor *with* Christ as a companion, not as a servile minion blindly following orders. This is a partnership

with Christ and, by extension, a collaborative enterprise with other disciples of Christ:

> If we give consideration to such a call from the temporal king to his subjects, how much *more* worthy of our consideration it is to gaze upon Christ our Lord, the eternal King, and all the world assembled before him. He calls to them all, and to each person in particular he says: "My will is to conquer the whole world and all my enemies, and thus to enter into the glory of my Father. Therefore, whoever wishes to come *with me* must labor *with me*, so that through following me in the pain he or she may follow me also in the glory." (*SE* 95, emphasis added)

Ignatius now suggests two responses. Both are loving responses of a generous disciple. The first response is the offering of a disciple who commits him- or herself wholeheartedly to the work of the kingdom of God:

> [I will reflect that] all those who have judgment and reason will offer themselves wholeheartedly for this labor. (*SE* 96)

This offering is a matter of reason and good judgment: it makes sense that if we are going to follow a noble, worldly leader, we will want to follow Christ all the more. The second offering suggests an even more generous, more heartfelt response. The disciple devotes him- or herself not simply to laboring for the kingdom but also to being with Christ and imitating more completely his way of living:

> Those who desire to show *greater* devotion and to distinguish themselves in *total* service to their eternal King and universal Lord, will not only

offer their persons for their labor, but *go further* still. They will work against their human sensitivities and against their carnal and worldly love, and they will make offerings of *greater* worth and moment, and say (*SE* 97, emphasis added):

"Eternal Lord of all things, I make my offering, with your favor and help. I make it in the presence of your infinite Goodness, and of your glorious Mother, and of all the holy men and women in your heavenly court. I wish and desire, and it is my deliberate decision, provided only that it is for your *greater* service and praise, to imitate you in bearing all injuries and affronts, and any poverty, actual as well as spiritual, if your Most Holy Majesty desires to choose and receive me into such a life and state." (*SE* 98, emphasis added)

Ask: *What desires, dreams, concerns, fears, or hopes does Christ's invitation stir in me? How am I moved to respond now?*

Day 3

Repetition. Ignatius suggests some responses to the call of Christ, but how would *you* respond in your own words, in all honesty, and in the context of your life now?

Day 4

Read Matthew 4:18–25 (call of the disciples). Consider Jesus' call and the response of the disciples.

Day 5

Read Matthew 3:13–17. Accompany Jesus to the Jordan River. Be with him during his baptism. See how the Holy Spirit is giving him a deeper sense of his own vocation. In a colloquy, share your hopes, dreams, and desires to follow his Spirit in your life.

Day 6

Read Isaiah 42:1–9 ("Here is my servant, whom I uphold"). What inspires you about the mission of a disciple? How are you called to be a servant?

Day 7

Savor the graces of the week.

For Further Reflection

There are so many world leaders whose words and actions inspire us to service and who can remind us of Christ's even greater summons. One of my favorite inspirations is from Theodore Roosevelt, who said this in a speech at the Sorbonne in 1910:

It is not the critic who counts; not the man who points out how the strong man stumbles, or where the doer of deeds could have done them better. The credit belongs to the man who is actually in the arena, whose face is marred by dust and sweat and blood; who strives valiantly; who errs, and comes short again and again, because there is no effort without error and shortcoming; but who does actually strive to do the deeds; who knows the great enthusiasms, the great devotions; who spends himself in a worthy cause; who at the best knows in the end the triumph of high achievement, and who at the worst, if he fails, at least fails while daring greatly, so that his place shall never be with those cold and timid souls who know neither victory nor defeat.

Poverty of Spirit

As WE SEE IN THE exercises on the call of Christ, our King, and in later exercises, the disciple of Christ aspires to poverty.

All of us are called to "poverty of spirit," or **spiritual poverty**, which describes a stance of utter dependence before God, not in any demeaning, servile sense, but in the sense of the Principle and Foundation: God is God, and we are creatures created to praise, love, and serve God. Before all else, we depend on God for our happiness and fulfillment. While we are grateful for our talents, abilities, wealth, and achievements, we are free enough to offer them to the service of God and others and to let go of them when they get in the way of that self-giving.

In short, poverty of spirit is an emptying of self so that God can fill us with life and love. Our prayer helps us grow in spiritual poverty and freedom. Christ is the model of spiritual poverty par excellence.

Christ also lived in actual or **material poverty**, with a lack of material goods. Some people may be called to this way of living. Priests, brothers, and sisters in religious orders profess a vow of poverty, renouncing personal possessions and wealth and depending on their religious community for their material needs. God may call others to a life of material poverty without professing vows. Material poverty is not an end in itself, for abject poverty is degrading to the human person (as a survey of our world so tragically reveals). Instead, for those called to this state of life, material poverty is a means to deepen one's commitment to the poor whom Christ held so dear.

Although not everyone is called to live a life of actual poverty, we are all called to live simply and in freedom with respect to the riches we have—whether they are in the form of material possessions, talents, reputation, or influence. All are called to labor with Christ to help the poor and powerless in some way. All are called to give countercultural witness to the rampant competition and materialism around us.

A Loving Disciple's Offering by Joseph Tetlow, SJ

Eternal Lord of all things,
I feel Your gaze on me.
I sense that Your Mother stands near,
and the great beings crowd around you,
angels and powers and martyrs and saints.
If You will help me, please,
I would like to make an offering:
I want it to be my desire, and my choice,
provided that You want it this way,
to walk this earth the way You walked it.
I know that You lived in a little town,
without luxury, without great education.
I know that You refused political power.
I know that You suffered: Leaders rejected you.
Friends abandoned You. You failed.
I know. I hate to think about it.
None of it looks romantic to me, or very useful.
But it seems to me a toweringly wonderful thing
that Your divine majesty might call me to follow after You.
Amen.

JOSEPH TETLOW, SJ, is a Jesuit of the New Orleans Province who has been a leader in promoting the Spiritual Exercises in daily life and in training others to offer the nineteenth-annotation retreat to diverse populations. His manual for directors, *Choosing Christ in the World*, has served as an invaluable resource for directors and retreatants for many years. This prayer paraphrases the offering of the loving disciple in the kingdom of Christ meditation.

Week of Prayer #16: Jesus' Public Ministry Begins

After his baptism, Jesus does not simply rest on the banks of the Jordan. The Gospel writers move us to the desert, where Jesus is tempted, and then to his public ministry. In the First Week of the Exercises, we encountered the reality of evil. Jesus does the same in the desert, although he does not submit to temptation as we often do.

Recall the fundamental grace of the Second Week: to know Jesus more intimately so that we can love him more dearly and follow him more closely. In order to know Jesus, we must take his humanity seriously (Jesus really was tempted). We must not forget that while he is fully divine, he is also fully human. To gloss over Jesus' humanity is to miss one of the central meanings of the Incarnation: Jesus shows us that the way to our divinity (or holiness) is through our humanity, not around it. In other words, Jesus teaches us how to be fully human. The more we, who are created in the image of God, embrace our humanity, with all of its beauty and limitations, the more our divinity is revealed—that is, the more like God we become.

The Gospel writers offer us different portraits of Jesus. During the retreat, we don't need to concern ourselves with questions of historical accuracy or discrepancies among the Gospels. Guided by the Spirit, the evangelists, writing decades after Jesus' life, death, and resurrection, present the truth of who Jesus is for them and for us. Enjoy these different perspectives. Pray that you become more like the One you gaze upon during these weeks.

✝ PRAYER FOR THE WEEK

I pray for the following grace: to know Jesus more intimately, to love him more intensely, and to follow him more closely.

DAY 1
Read Matthew 4:1–11. Be with Jesus as he is tempted in the desert. Talk to him in a colloquy. (Recall Hebrews 4:14–16: Jesus Christ sympathizes with our weaknesses because he experienced testing, though without sin.)

DAY 2
Read Luke 4:14–30. Accompany Jesus as he experiences rejection from the people of his own town.

DAY 3
Read Mark 1:21–39. Join Jesus on a busy day.

DAY 4
Repetition of any passage.

DAY 5
Read Mark 2:1–12 (cure of the paralytic). Imagine carrying a friend to Jesus, or being carried by your friends to him.

DAY 6
Application of the five senses (p. 140) to any meditation this week.

DAY 7
Savor the graces of the week.

For Further Reflection

The laborers in the Lord's vineyard should have one foot on the ground, and the other raised to proceed on their journey.

—St. Ignatius of Loyola, in *Thoughts of St. Ignatius Loyola for Every Day of the Year*

Rules for Discernment of Spirits: Dealing with Spiritual Desolation

IN THE RULES FOR DISCERNMENT of Spirits, Ignatius devotes more time to desolation than to consolation because, quite simply, people need more help in times of desolation than in times of consolation. When we become aware that we are in the midst of desolation, Ignatius suggests the following four ways of thinking or acting:

> 1. During a time of desolation one should never make a change. Instead, one should remain firm and constant in the resolutions and in the decision which one had on the day before the desolation, or in a decision in which one was during a previous time of consolation. For just as the good spirit is chiefly the one who guides and counsels us in time of consolation, so it is the evil spirit who does this in time of desolation. By following his counsels we can never find the way to a right decision. (*SE* 318)

Remember that the evil spirit wants nothing more than to get us off track as we grow in faith, hope, and love. Thus, if we made a good decision in a time of consolation, then we should resist changing it, which can be very tempting to do in times of desolation. Hold your ground. Only when the desolation passes should we reconsider a decision already made.

2. Although we ought not to change our former resolutions in time of desolation, it is very profitable to make vigorous changes in ourselves against the desolation, for example, by insisting more on prayer, meditation, earnest self-examination, or some suitable way of doing penance. (*SE* 319)

Although we should not change decisions or make new decisions while in desolation, we should not be entirely passive in the face of the enemy's seductions. We can fight back by making sure our house is in order. Remain faithful to prayer. Talk to a trusted spiritual mentor. Do a penance, which may be a small act of self-denial or a more positive act of caring for yourself or someone else. Do anything that will help you remember God's faithfulness and your goodness.

3. When we are in desolation we should think that the Lord has left us to our own powers in order to test us, so that we may prove ourselves by resisting the various agitations and temptations of the enemy. For we can do this with God's help, which always remains available, even if we do not clearly perceive it. Indeed, even though the Lord has withdrawn from us his abundant fervor, augmented love, and intensive grace, he still supplies sufficient grace for our eternal salvation. (*SE* 320)

In desolation, we may feel that God has abandoned us, but that is not the case. God is faithful and remains with us; however, the good feelings of spiritual consolation are gone for the time being. Such times provide the opportunity to strengthen ourselves against temptation by resisting the enemy's seductions. This will make it easier to deal with such temptations the next time around. Also, by remaining faithful in difficult times, we come to understand that faith involves more than feeling good; faith has to do with steadfast commitment, which deepens our friendship with God.

> 4. One who is in desolation should strive to preserve himself or herself in patience. This is the counterattack against the vexations which are being experienced. One should remember that after a while the consolation will return again, through the diligent efforts against the desolation which were suggested in [number 2]. (*SE* 321)

Here Ignatius offers some very practical advice: be patient. Hang in there, and don't lose perspective. Consolation will come again, with your own efforts and with the help of God. Recall that in a prior rule, Ignatius advised that we store up consolations for times of desolation that will naturally come. Remembering those past consolations will help us remain patient. We are reassured that this difficult time will pass and that consolation will be ours again. In the midst of desolation, we can hope, thus dispelling the darkness.

In his artfully written guide to Ignatian discernment, *God's Voice Within*, Mark Thibodeaux, SJ, offers a helpful image that reinforces these points. Being human, we naturally deal with various disturbances of the soul. We can't help but feel hurt, jealous, angry, or tempted sometimes. The challenge is that as we discern where these feelings come from, we do not indulge them nor get too distracted by them. If we are attentive enough, we notice that these feelings come and go. So imagine, as Mark did, that you are on a long bus ride, and a variety of people end up sitting in the seat next to you, getting on and off at different stops along the way. That's the way anger—or any other emotion—is sometimes; it comes and goes. So when anger comes, let it sit quietly next to you, and be attentive to it, but certainly don't let it get in the driver's seat. You know that in time it will get off the bus. The rules for discernment teach us how we can nurture a quietness or equilibrium of soul that helps us see those desolations and distractions for what they are—parts of us, but not defining us.

Week of Prayer #17:
Meditation on Two
Standards

THIS WEEK, WE PRAY WITH another key exercise: the **Two Standards**. Ignatius, a man of his times, borrows from his military past to construct this meditation. A standard is a banner or flag under which the followers of a particular leader rally. Ignatius asks us to consider the opposing tactics and values of Christ and Lucifer (also known in the language of the Exercises as the enemy of our human nature, the father of lies, the evil one, the deceiver). We are asked to choose the banner under which we will stand.

At first, it seems like an easy choice—who wouldn't choose Christ? But as we learned in the First Week of the Exercises, the strategies of the enemy are subtle. The enemy begins by seducing us with riches. Such riches can win for us honors and the esteem of others, which we can begin to excessively desire. Fixation on riches and honors devolves into a self-serving pride, leaving little room for God or anyone else. In *Making Choices in Christ*, Joseph Tetlow, SJ distills the enemy's tactics to these exclamations: "Look at all this stuff I have!" leads to "Look at me with all this stuff" and finally "Look at *me!*" (p. 108).

The strategy of Christ is the opposite. We embrace the counter-cultural values of poverty, self-giving, and dignified humility. The poverty of Christ is both spiritual and material. Spiritually poor, Jesus relies on the Father's love and support. Materially poor, he chooses to live with few possessions. His poverty allows him to live for others more easily. Imitating Christ in this way, we, too, live with meaning, dignity, and joy.

Material wealth is not in itself an evil, but the wisdom of the Gospels and great sages—not to mention our own experience—teaches us that with wealth come temptations and distractions. As a self-check, we can ask: *Am I generous with my wealth? Is my wealth getting in the way of other priorities in my life? How attached am I to what I have? Does what I have define who I am? Do the poor and forgotten have a place in my life?*

The words *pride* and *humility* can be applied falsely. False pride and humility are tools of the enemy, for they foster self-involvement. False pride puts me at the center of the universe, whereas false humility beats me up through shame and self-hatred. In contrast, Christ-like pride recognizes the truth that each person is created in the image of God and enjoys inherent dignity. Persons with Christ-like humility acknowledge their worth as human beings but also recognize their human limitations. Such persons are grateful for the gifts of God. They know who they are, with all of their beauty and blemishes.

By becoming more aware of the enemy's tactics, we deepen our understanding of the Rules for the Discernment of Spirits. Such awareness helps us hear and respond to the call of Christ, the King, and fosters the interior freedom described in the Principle and Foundation.

✝ Prayer for the Week

I pray for the following graces: an awareness of the enemy's deceits and courage in the face of them; an understanding of Christ's way of living and a desire to live that way.

Day 1

Meditation on Two Standards (*SE* 136–48): We begin this meditation by imagining the setting of our choice between the two standards. In the end, there is no middle ground: we must choose.

> Here it will be to imagine a great plain in the region of Jerusalem, where the supreme commander of the good people is Christ our Lord; then another plain in the region of Babylon, where the leader of the enemy is Lucifer. (*SE* 138)

In other words, we imagine a place that is peaceful, just, and beautiful, and another place that's full of corruption. Feel free to imagine places like these in the world today.

Next, we meditate on the two standards, beginning with the standard of the enemy:

> Imagine the leader of all the enemy in that great plain of Babylon. He is seated on a throne of fire and smoke, in aspect horrible and terrifying. (*SE* 140)

> Consider how he summons uncountable devils, disperses some to one city and others to another, and thus throughout the whole world, without missing any provinces, places, states, or individual persons. (*SE* 141)

> Consider the address he makes to them: How he admonishes them to set up snares and chains; how first they should tempt people to covet riches (as he usually does, at least in most cases), so that they may more easily come to vain honor from the world, and finally to surging pride. In this way, the first step is riches, the second is

honor, and the third is pride; and from these three steps the enemy entices them to all the other vices. (*SE* 142)

Ignatius's language reflects his medieval imagination. If such descriptions are not helpful to you, use your imagination to construct a modern-day setting for the meditation. Pay attention to your affective or emotional reactions when praying.

DAY 2

Meditation on Two Standards, continued. We now consider the standard of Christ, who stands in stark contrast to Lucifer. Although the enemy is repulsive, harsh, and seeks only to deceive and enslave people, Christ is inviting, gentle, and desires only to liberate people to love God and serve others. Both want to rule the world, but in different ways and for different reasons. Listen to Christ's invitation. Gaze upon him as he speaks to his disciples. Feel free to imagine a modern-day setting for the parable:

> In contrast, gaze in imagination on the supreme and true leader, who is Christ our Lord. (*SE* 143) Consider how Christ our Lord takes his place in that great plain near Jerusalem, in an area which is lowly, beautiful, and attractive. (*SE* 144)

> Consider how the Lord of all the world chooses so many persons, apostles, disciples, and the like. He sends them throughout the whole world, to spread his doctrine among people of every state and condition. (*SE* 145)

> Consider the address that Christ our Lord makes to all his servants and friends whom he is

sending on this expedition. He recommends that they endeavor to aid all persons, by attracting them, first, to the most perfect spiritual poverty and also, if the Divine Majesty should be served and should wish to choose them for it, even to no less a degree of actual poverty; and second, by attracting them to a desire of reproaches and contempt, since from these results humility.

In this way there will be three steps: the first, poverty in opposition to riches; the second, reproaches or contempt in opposition to honor from the world; and the third, humility in opposition to pride. Then from these three steps they should induce people to all the other virtues. (*SE* 146)

Recall that all of us are called to spiritual poverty, to a greater reliance on God. As for material poverty and other sacrifices, including being misunderstood by others, we don't seek or accept these as ends in themselves, but only if God calls us to embrace them as part of living our faith. Thus, Ignatius provides the condition: we accept them only if "the Divine Majesty should be served and should wish to choose them for it."

Day 3

Repetition. Consider: *How do I experience the two standards playing out in my life or in the world around me? What role do riches and honors play in my life? What enslaves me? Where is the invitation to greater freedom in my life?*

Conclude your prayer with a triple colloquy, which underscores how serious and sometimes difficult the choice between the two standards actually is. The grace we ask for is a gift.

We need God's help to live so focused on Christ, to live so counterculturally, and to live in such a way that we freely accept riches or poverty, honors or insults.

In the colloquy, we first ask Mary, mother of God and our mother, "to obtain for me grace from her Son and Lord that I may be received under his standard"; next, "ask the same grace from the Son, that he may obtain it for me from the Father"; and then "ask the same grace from the Father, that he may grant it to me" (*SE* 147). Conclude with a Hail Mary, an Our Father, or the *Anima Christi* (pp. 41–42).

Day 4

Read Matthew 4:23–5:12. The beatitudes express the standard of Christ. Imagine that you are present in the crowd or with the disciples, watching and listening to Jesus. Allow his manner and words to affect you.

Day 5

Read Luke 18:18–30 (the danger of riches and the rewards of generosity). Remember that it is not wealth itself that is evil but excessively desiring wealth and misusing it at the expense of others. Try to appreciate the effect that desiring riches, power, or control has on individual lives and in societies with unjust distributions of wealth.

Day 6

Repetition of one of the previous days' Scripture passages. Or Matthew 11:28–30 ("Take my yoke upon you, and learn from me").

Day 7

Savor the graces of the week.

For Further Reflection

Solidarity is the social meaning of humility. Just as humility leads individuals to all other virtues, humility as solidarity is the foundation of a just society. In short, the standard of Christ today is **downward mobility**. That means entering the world of the poor, assuming their cause, and to some degree, their condition.

Solidarity shapes our lifestyle, which will depend on each one's vocation. Solidarity doesn't necessarily mean destitution. It has nothing to do with denying our training or neglecting our talents. Special obligations, for example, to family and benefactors, carry weight in deliberating about lifestyle. We should beware of dogmatizing about having a car or a computer, about whether to save for old age or where to educate our children. These are legitimate matters for **discernment**, but not for one-size-fits-all formulas.

At the same time, the objective criterion of our poverty is **solidarity with the poor**. We will feel uncomfortable with superfluities when poor friends lack essentials. Attachment to them will detach us from luxuries, and even necessities. As the New Testament and Christian tradition tell us, possessions are resources entrusted to us, to be administered for the good of all, especially those in need. This logic extends to other resources. What about pursuing higher education in a world of hunger? If we have that opportunity, then studying means storing up cultural capital to be administered later on behalf of those who need us.

How much should we have? Better to reframe the question: Do we feel at home among the poor? Do they feel comfortable in our homes? Or do our furnishings and possessions make them feel like unimportant people?

Solidarity leads to sharing the obscurity, misunderstanding, and contempt experienced by the poor. Assuming their cause will most likely bring the world's ridicule and fury down on our heads. We might even feel left out if our friends suffer these things and we do not.

Week of Prayer #18:
The Call and Cost of Discipleship

The Meditation on Two Standards stirs in us noble desires to serve and follow Christ in his simplicity of life, his humility, and his selflessness. It presents an ideal way of living. Now we do a reality check of sorts. We know the allure of the call of Christ, but we also grapple with the demands of discipleship. In all our choices, we want to choose the *magis*, "to choose that which is more to the glory of the Divine Majesty and the salvation of my soul" (*SE* 152).

Recall from the Principle and Foundation that in making choices we strive for **indifference**: we want to be free enough from our disordered loves and fears to respond wholeheartedly to God's call and choose whatever leads to God's greater glory and the service of others. Responding to the call of Christ is not always easy. While our culture prizes radical individualism, self-indulgence, and quick fixes, Jesus reveals self-giving as the way to a new life of community, true freedom, and joy beyond our imagining.

Desiring to know and love Jesus more so that we can follow him more faithfully, we understand that love is more than a feeling; feelings come and go. Love is a decision, a commitment to live for another. The sacrifice that discipleship sometimes entails makes sense only when done out of love.

✝ Prayer for the Week

I pray for the following grace: to grow in interior freedom so that I'm able to respond wholeheartedly to Christ's invitation in my life.

Day 1

Read John 21:15–19. Imagine this colloquy between the risen Christ and Peter. Hear the invitation and the response. Imagine the same invitation to you. How do you respond? How do you react to the cost of discipleship?

Day 2

Meditation on the Three Classes of Persons (*SE* 149–57). In this meditation, we reflect on concrete choices that three different types of persons may make as they try to live according to their calling in life. In doing so, we experience some tension between the high ideals of Christ's call and our lack of interior freedom and deeply embedded resistances to Christ's invitation to us personally.

Imagine that the three persons are good people (like us) who are trying to serve God and grow in faith. They sincerely want nothing to get in the way of their relationship with God.

Imagine that each acquires something that is very attractive to him or her. Ignatius suggests a large amount of money, but you can imagine something especially attractive to you, such as a certain material possession, a place to live, a high-profile job, or a particular honor. None of these things is intrinsically evil; each one can be used for good. But each of the three typical persons is excessively attached to the possession in some way. This preoccupation risks getting in the way of a greater good or a more generous response to God's call.

Imagine each of the three persons:

- **The one who procrastinates.** The first person feels a growing attachment to her possession and is concerned that her dependence on it may interfere with giving her life wholeheartedly to God. So she wants to let go of the attachment, but she clutters her life with so many other things and things to do that she never gets around to it. Even on her deathbed, she is still thinking about letting go of her attachment.

- **The one who compromises.** Like the first person, the second person worries that he is becoming too attached to a certain possession. He sincerely desires to be free of that excessive preoccupation; at the same time, he wants to keep the possession. So he does lots of good things and makes honorable sacrifices, but he fails to do the one thing that he really needs to do: free himself from his disordered attachment. In a sense, this person is trying to negotiate with God. Rather than conforming his will to God's will, the compromiser wants God to do what he wants to do. In avoiding the difficult choice, the second person remains unfree with respect to the possession.

- **The one who is truly free or indifferent.** In Ignatius's words:

> The person typical of the third class desires to get rid of the attachment, but in such a way that there remains no inclination either to keep the acquired money or to dispose of it. Instead such a one desires to keep it or reject it solely according to what God our Lord will move one's will to choose, and also according to what the person himself or herself will judge to be better for the service and praise of the Divine Majesty. (*SE* 155)

Note where the third person begins: she is not sure whether or not God is asking her to give up the possession; she simply desires to be free to do what God wants her to do. So she begins by asking God what she should do. She is open to how God directs her through her prayer, her experience, her reasoning through different options, her discernment of consolations and desolations, and the wise counsel of others.

The truly free person checks her motivations, which are often mixed. She tries to choose from a desire to better serve God and others. The third person may feel some attachment to the possession and does not mind waiting to make a decision. But she does not procrastinate. She does make a timely decision (acknowledging that we rarely reach complete indifference).

With respect to the attachments in your life and the choices you have made, how have you resembled the three persons: the procrastinator, the compromiser, and the truly free person?

Day 3

Read Mark 10:17–31 (Jesus calls the rich man to follow him). Imagine this scene. Notice the rich man's noble desires but also his lack of interior freedom because of his excessive attachments. Look at Jesus looking upon him *with love.* Hear Jesus' words of encouragement to Peter and to you. Ask: *What attachments or disordered loves are getting in the way of my responding to Christ's invitation?*

Day 4

Read Mark 12:41–44 (the widow's offering). Watch as the widow gives everything she has; marvel at her freedom. Ask: *How have I demonstrated such freedom in my life with respect to money, possessions, priorities, work, or time?*

Day 5

Repetition of any of the previous days.

Day 6

Read Matthew 16:24–26 (Jesus speaks of discipleship). Ask: *How do I react to the demands of discipleship? How have I found new life by offering myself to others?*

Day 7

Savor the graces of the week.

For Further Reflection

The entire life of a good Christian is an exercise in holy desire. You do not see what you long for, but the very act of desiring prepares you, so that when God comes you may see and be utterly satisfied.

Suppose you are going to fill some holder or container, and you know you will be given a large amount. Then you set about stretching your sack or wineskin or whatever it is. Why? Because you know the quantity you will have to put in it, and your eyes tell you there is not enough room. By stretching it, therefore, you increase the capacity of the sack, and this is how God deals with us. Simply by making us wait, God increases our desire, which in turn enlarges the capacity of our soul, making it able to receive what is to be given to us.

These are the words of St. Augustine, in a homily on the first letter of John.

Rules for Discernment of Spirits: Reasons We Experience Desolation

IN THE SPIRITUAL LIFE, WE naturally experience periods of consolation and desolation. God, who loves us and wants us to grow in faith, hope, and love, gifts us with consolation. God does not inflict desolation on us but does permit it to happen.

Ignatius suggests three main causes for the spiritual desolation we suffer. His hope is that the more we understand these reasons, the less likely we are to become mired in the unpleasant feelings associated with spiritual desolation.

> 1. The first is that we ourselves are tepid, lazy, or negligent in our spiritual exercises. Thus the spiritual consolation leaves us because of our own faults. (*SE* 322)

Spiritual desolation is a wake-up call when we have been lax in our spiritual exercise or have settled for shallowness in our prayer. Review again the suggestions for prayer in the introduction of this book. Follow Ignatius's counsels on prayer and the advice of a wise spiritual guide. Commit yourself with renewed vigor to the church's liturgy and sacraments and to service of people who are in need.

> 2. The second is that the desolation is meant to test how much we are worth and how far we will extend ourselves in the service and praise of God, even without much repayment by way of consolations and increased graces. (*SE* 322)

Spiritual desolation is not always our fault. Sometimes God permits it so that we can learn more about ourselves and our God. We discover what our faith is all about. As David Fleming asks when interpreting this rule, do we love God or do we just love the gifts of God?

Love for God or another person is more than just a feeling; it's a decision and a commitment. Our love for God deepens when we commit to God in both good times and in bad, when we experience feelings of intimacy and closeness and when such consoling feelings are absent. When we resist temptations and persist in the hope that God is with us, we demonstrate faithfulness and thus use these opportunities for spiritual growth.

> 3. The third is that the desolation is meant to give us a true recognition and understanding, so that we may perceive interiorly that we cannot by ourselves bring on or retain great devotion, intense love, tears, or any other spiritual consolation, but that all these are a gift and grace from God our Lord; and further, to prevent us from building our nest in a house which belongs to Another, by puffing up our minds with pride or vainglory through which we attribute to ourselves the devotion or other features of spiritual consolation. (*SE* 322)

Times of spiritual desolation are exercises in humility; they remind us that we cannot make, summon, or control grace. Consolation is a gift from God, which we can take for granted when things are going well. In desolation, we are reminded of our spiritual poverty—our constant need for God.

WEEK OF PRAYER #19:
THREE WAYS OF LOVING

PRAYING THROUGH THE EXERCISES IS usually not a linear progression, with graces experienced in a neat, sequential flow. Rather, think of the Exercises as an ever-deepening spiral of grace. We keep returning to key graces and insights, meditations and contemplations, desires and reasonings, savoring each, going deeper and deeper into the mystery of who God is and who we are before God.

In the Contemplation on the Call of Christ, our King, we heard Christ's call to labor with him on mission. This week, we continue to gaze at him, appreciating what this mission is all about. In the Meditation on Two Standards, we considered how Jesus goes about his mission in poverty, humility, and self-giving. In the Meditation on Three Classes of Persons, we reflected on the interior freedom and commitment necessary to follow Jesus more closely. All these meditations take us back to the beginning, to the Principle and Foundation, which reminds us to keep focused on our most basic mission: to praise, love, and serve God.

In this week, we pray through another meditation, the **Three Kinds of Humility**, which deepens the graces asked for in the previous mediations. Remember that Christian humility is not about demeaning yourself; hating the self is a failure to honor the goodness of God's creation in us. Authentic humility is a way of loving God and ourselves. A humble person recognizes his or her need and dependence on God, and thus is another expression of spiritual poverty. A humble person embraces the liberating truth of our humanity: we are not the center of the universe—God is! Authentic humility helps us rejoice in who we are and Whose we are, with all of our gifts and limitations.

The three kinds of humility are really just three ways or degrees of loving God. Remember that for Ignatius, the *magis*, the "more," is always important: we strive for the *greater* way of loving. In this striving, notice whether you find yourself resisting Jesus' invitation. If so, pay attention to where the resistance lies.

✝ Prayer for the Week

I pray for the following grace: to know Jesus more intimately, to love him more intensely, and to follow him more closely.

Day 1
Read Luke 19:1–10 (Jesus calls Zacchaeus). Imagine this scene. Jesus loves by reaching out to those on the margins: "The Son of Man came to seek out and to save the lost." Notice how Jesus loves the tax collector.

Day 2
Read Luke 7:1–10 (cure of centurion's servant). Jesus loves by caring for the needs of people who come his way. Notice how Jesus cares for the centurion and his servant. Bring your own needs to Jesus. Notice also how free the centurion is—a Roman soldier and non-Jew who is benevolent with his own authority and respectful of Jesus' authority.

Day 3
Read Mark 5:21–43 (cure of the woman with hemorrhage; daughter of Jairus raised to life). How does Jesus love those he meets in these scenes? Do you identify with anyone in the scenes?

Day 4

Repetition of any of the previous Scripture passages. Remember to include a colloquy in your prayer.

Day 5

Three Kinds of Humility (*SE* 165–68). Ignatius invites us to consider three kinds of humility, which lie on a spectrum of varying degrees of loving God:

In the first kind of humility, we express our love for God by doing our duty and following God's law. We avoid grave sin, for we don't want to do anything that would separate us from God. We love God as our Creator, as Lord of the Universe, but this love may be hindered by fear and excessive caution in acting.

In the second (and "more perfect") kind of humility, as in the first, we love God by honoring God's law and avoiding sin. But we also strive for indifference. We cultivate an attitude of interior freedom, finding a balance in our desires and attachments so that we will follow what God wants for us. We exercise good judgment and monitor our motivations carefully. We are enamored of Christ's vision for us and our world, yet we tend to keep a respectful distance. We are zealous but our response, though sincere, is not yet wholehearted.

In the third (and "most perfect") kind of humility, we move beyond following God's law and making reasoned judgments—both good things—and we experience a heartfelt desire to imitate Christ more closely. We do not hold back. We simply want to be where Jesus is, no matter the cost. In Ignatius's words:

> When the options equally further the praise and
> glory of God, in order to imitate Christ our Lord
> better and to be more like him here and now,
> I desire and choose poverty with Christ poor
> rather than wealth; contempt with Christ laden

with it rather than honors. Even further, I desire
to be regarded as a useless fool for Christ, who
before me was regarded as such, rather than as a
wise or prudent person in this world. (*SE* 167)

In this third way of loving, we pray for the desire to experience in our life what Jesus experienced in his. We do not seek poverty, contempt, or foolishness for its own sake but to become more united with Jesus Christ, whom we love. Out of love, we desire so much to be with Christ and to live according to his values (his "standard") that we accept whatever comes with our commitment. We become indifferent to results as the world judges them. The third kind of humility reminds us how countercultural the gospel can be. Loving in any of these ways—but especially in the third, wholeheartedly—is a gift from God.

Ask: *How have I loved in the degrees described in the Meditation on the Three Kinds of Humility?*

Day 6

Read Mark 12:28–34. Listen to Jesus articulate the great commandments to love. Review the third way of loving. Pray for the grace to love in this way. Ask: *Have I seen such loving in my life? How do I resist loving or being loved?*

Day 7

Repetition of any day.

For Further Reflection

The saint is unlike everybody else precisely because he is humble. . . . Humility consists in being precisely the person you actually are before God, and since no two people are alike, if you have the humility to be yourself you will not be like anyone else in the whole universe. . . .

A humble man is not disturbed by praise. Since he is no longer concerned with himself, and since he knows where the good that is in him comes from, he does not refuse praise, because it belongs to the God he loves, and in receiving it he keeps nothing for himself but gives it all, and with great joy, to God.

—Thomas Merton, *New Seeds of Contemplation*

WEEK OF PRAYER #20: JESUS' PUBLIC MINISTRY

WE CONTINUE TO PRAY THROUGH Jesus' public ministry. Keep your eyes and heart fixed on Jesus. Use your imagination to become part of these Gospel scenes. In a colloquy, speak with Jesus or another person in the scene.

There's no need now to make any big decisions and commitments about how specifically you will follow Christ's call in your life. If you need to make such a decision, it is best to make it only after getting to know better the One who calls you. Our hope is simply that we become more like the One who is the focus of our attention. We want to see, hear, speak, and feel as Jesus does.

Continue to be aware of the areas in your life in which you experience greater freedom and in which some disordered loves linger.

The practice of a daily Examen is very helpful in ongoing discernment and growth in freedom.

✝ PRAYER FOR THE WEEK

I pray for the following grace: to know Jesus more intimately, to love him more intensely, and to follow him more closely.

DAY 1
Read John 2:1–11 (wedding feast at Cana).

Day 2

Read Mark 8:22–26 (healing of blind man at Bethsaida).

Day 3

Read Luke 17:11–19 (the grateful leper).

Day 4

Repetition of one of the previous Scripture passages.

Day 5

Read Luke 10:38–42 (Martha and Mary).

Day 6

Read Mark 10:13–16 (Jesus and children).

Day 7

Savor the graces of the week. Review your journal or return to one of the Scripture passages here.

Rules for Discernment of Spirits: Three Metaphors for How the Enemy Acts in Our Lives

IGNATIUS DISCERNED THAT THE EVIL spirit works in typical ways. He proposes three metaphors for how the evil spirit acts: a spoiled child, a false lover, and a military commander.* If we are aware of the evil spirit's movement, then we can act against temptations, seductive lies, and deceptions. Reflect on how the evil spirit has worked on you in these ways, and recall examples of how you reacted. Such understanding will strengthen you in future spiritual struggles.

The Enemy Behaves Like a Spoiled Child

When an adult is firm with a petulant child, the child usually gives up. But if an adult starts to indulge a quarreling child or shows weakness in any way, the child becomes even bolder and more unyielding in his or her demands. Ignatius continues:

---

*In the original text of the Exercises, Ignatius first compares the evil spirit to a woman who quarrels with an adversary and then to a man ("a scoundrel") who seduces a woman and then tries to hide the affair. Such analogies rightfully offend modern sensibilities and actually betray Ignatius's own esteem for the women and men with whom he labored and shared the Exercises. Following the lead of David Fleming, SJ, I replace the image of a quarreling woman with a spoiled child and make the false lover either a man or a woman. Central to understanding the rule is not the age or gender of the proposed person but their behavior. I retain the third image of the military commander.

> In the same way, the enemy characteristically weakens, loses courage, and flees with his temptations when the person engaged in spiritual endeavors stands bold and unyielding against the enemy's temptations and goes diametrically against them. But if, in contrast, that person begins to fear and lose courage in the face of the temptations, there is no beast on the face of the earth as fierce as the enemy of human nature when he is pursuing his damnable intention with his surging malice. (*SE* 325)

The underlying assumption of this rule is that the evil spirit is basically weak. Although the enemy may tempt us, we can resist. In the face of our strength, the enemy cowers. So when we are tempted to sin or to act in a way that gets in the way of loving God, self, or others, we should do exactly the opposite of what the evil spirit wants us to do. This is usually an act of will or sheer determination. We may not feel like resisting the temptation because it is so alluring and pleasing.

Gordon Bennett, SJ, was my spiritual director at a time when I was confronting a pattern of recurrent worries about the future. They were distractions from the joy I was experiencing in my present work and life as a Jesuit. He offered an image that helped me understand this particular rule for discernment. Imagine, he suggested, that you are on a subway platform. The subway arrives at the station, and the doors open. Imagine that inside the subway car are all those distracting feelings and preoccupations begging to be indulged. But just hold your ground, he told me. Keep your feet firmly planted on the platform because you know that the doors will close and that train will move on, without you on it.

Ignatius cautions that we must act against the temptations as soon as they begin, otherwise they can easily wear us down, much like a spoiled child can. Twelve-step programs offer some helpful advice to all of us. Be careful when you are hungry, angry, lonely, or tired (HALT). At such times, we are particularly vulnerable to the wiles of the evil spirit.

The Enemy Operates Like a False Lover, One Who Uses Another Person for His or Her Own Ends

Selfish people try to keep their machinations hidden. If a relationship is illicit, they will insist that the relationship not be disclosed or made public. False lovers want their duplicity kept secret so that they can continue unabated on their destructive course. Ignatius continues:

> In a similar manner, when the enemy of human nature turns his wiles and persuasions upon an upright person, he intends and desires them to be received and kept in secrecy. But when the person reveals them to his or her good confessor or some other spiritual person who understands the enemy's deceits and malice, he is grievously disappointed. For he quickly sees that he cannot succeed in the malicious project he began, because his manifest deceptions have been detected. (*SE* 326)

The evil spirit sows needless doubts, confusion, insecurities, anxiety, and various temptations and wants nothing more than for the person to keep these hidden, for in the darkness they will fester even more. But God always wants to bring light into the darkness.

To cooperate with this offer of grace, we must first become aware of the darkness within, which we can gloss over easily by avoiding prayer or by unnecessarily cluttering our life with noise, work, and other distractions. Once aware, we can certainly bring our need for healing and strength to God in prayer. We also benefit from talking to someone else about our experience of desolation.

This can be difficult because when we're in desolation we may not feel like talking to anyone, or we may be afraid of another's reaction, or we may doubt that others want to listen to us. Freeing ourselves of the burden of silence can be a courageous choice. Pray that trust displaces your fears.

Be prudent about the timing of such disclosure and how much to disclose. Be gentle with yourself. Ignatius is also clear that we should not talk to just anybody but to a wise and trusted guide who is adept in spiritual matters.

Sometimes, what we bring to the light may touch on matters that require the help of a therapist or psychologist. In such cases, a skilled spiritual director or confessor will know his or her limits and refer you to someone else so that your healing may continue.

The Enemy Acts Like a Military Commander, Mercilessly Pursuing an Objective in Battle

A military commander shrewdly assesses the strengths and weaknesses of his opponent and then attacks at the most vulnerable point. He or she searches out the opponent's blind spots or any point of unpreparedness. When the opponent becomes too self-satisfied and lets down his guard, the commander begins the assault. Ignatius continues:

> In the same way, the enemy of human nature prowls around and from every side probes all our theological, cardinal, and moral virtues. Then at the point where he finds us weakest and most in need in regard to our eternal salvation, there he attacks and tries to take us. (*SE* 327)

In the previous two images, Ignatius advises us about how to act when we discern the presence of the evil spirit: resist temptations from a position of strength, and bring secrets and gnawing desolation to the light. Here, he suggests that we fortify our weakness *before* the enemy's onslaught. To do this, we must be self-aware and honest with ourselves: *When am I am most susceptible to desolation? Which people, places, things, situations, or activities bring about interior desolation?* We look for patterns or habits that need to be undone with God's grace and our own effort. A daily Examen is an effective tool to grow in self-awareness.

In our vulnerability, we are likely to cry out for help to God or to other people. However, when we are complacent or too proud, we can become slack in our vigilance and easily forget our need for help, which is just what the evil spirit wants. Without a healthy humility, we may ignore our weaknesses and sin and open the door to desolation.

Remember Ignatius's fundamental premise: the enemy is weak, and grace always prevails, if we let it. With the gift of self-awareness, we can fortify our all-too-human weaknesses. The temptations, doubts, and fears may come, but they will not be able to take hold if grace leaves them no room.

Week of Prayer #21:
The Kingdom of God

In the Contemplation on the Call of Christ, our King, we heard the invitation to labor with Christ in building a more loving, just, and gentle world. In his teaching, Jesus invites us to imagine God's dream for the world. In his actions, Jesus shows us what the reign of God looks like concretely. As you pray this week, ask: *How does the call of Christ move me now? What bold, holy desires does Jesus' view of God's kingdom stir in me?*

The kingdom of God is not simply what awaits us in heaven at some time in the future. By becoming one of us in Christ, God revealed how the kingdom of God breaks into history, here and now. The kingdom of God is not a place but a way of living and being.

The *United States Catholic Catechism for Adults* beautifully describes the kingdom of God revealed in Jesus Christ:

> It is a Kingdom of love, justice, and mercy, where sins are forgiven, the sick are made whole, enemies are reconciled, captives are freed, and the needs of the poor are met.

> It is all these things and more, for ultimately the Kingdom is Jesus Christ and all he means for us. The Kingdom is already here because of the redemption of Jesus Christ. But in another sense, it is "not yet" here, since Christ's final

transformation of individuals, society, and culture has yet to happen in its fullness. This is why we need to pray this petition ["Thy Kingdom come"] every day and work for its coming.

✝ Prayer for the Week

I pray for the following grace: to know Jesus more intimately, to love him more intensely, and to follow him more closely.

Day 1
Read Luke 6:27–38 (Jesus teaches about the kingdom of God). Perhaps focus on just one particular teaching in this rich passage and try to apply it to your life.

Day 2
Read Luke 9:10–17 (Jesus feeds us: mind, body, and soul). Notice in the feeding of the five thousand how much Jesus does with what we consider so little. Notice, too, how he relies on the disciples to help him do the feeding. Finally, listen to the echoes of the Eucharist as Jesus takes, blesses, breaks, and gives the bread.

Day 3
Read Luke 10:25–37 (parable of the Good Samaritan). In this famous parable, we learn what mercy is all about. Compassion first involves noticing people in need and then acting out of that compassion in some effective way. In other words, what we see moves our mind and heart, which then moves our hands, feet, and mouth to help. How does this parable apply to a situation in your life or in our world?

Day 4
Repetition of one of the Scripture passages from days 1–3.

Day 5

Read Luke 13:10–17 (Jesus heals a crippled woman). Notice Jesus' compassionate response to the woman in comparison with the small-mindedness of the religious leaders. Are there long-suffering people in your life who need your care? Have you ever reacted as Jesus' opponents do here?

Day 6

Read Luke 12:22–32 ("Do not worry about your life. . . . Strive for [God's] kingdom").

Day 7

Savor the graces of the week. Review your journal or return to one of the Scripture passages from the previous days.

A Prayer by St. Teresa of Ávila

Let nothing disturb you,
Nothing frighten you;
All things are passing;
God never changes;
Patient endurance attains all things;
Whoever possesses God is wanting in nothing;
God alone suffices.

TERESA OF ÁVILA (1515–1582), a contemporary of St. Ignatius, helped to reform the Carmelite order, along with St. John of the Cross. Both visionaries believed that the best way to reform the church and to combat heresy was through a renewed commitment to holiness. Teresa's writings about prayer and the spiritual life have been read through the centuries. Her more popular writings include *The Way of Perfection* and *The Interior Castle*. Pope Paul VI named her a doctor of the church in 1970; she was the first woman to enjoy that distinction.

Week of Prayer #22:
Jesus as Human and
Divine

THE CHURCH HAS LONG TAUGHT that Jesus Christ is fully human and fully divine. As fully human, Jesus is like us in all things but sin. As fully divine, Jesus shows us who God is most completely. To be faithful to this teaching, we must avoid two extremes: emphasizing the humanity of Jesus so much that he becomes just another admirable human being or emphasizing the divinity of Jesus so much that he becomes otherworldly and inaccessible to us.

Although we tend to put humanity and divinity in separate categories, Jesus shows us that they are one. Remember one of the central insights of the Second Week: the path to divinity is *through* our humanity, not around it. In the Meditation on Two Standards, Ignatius refers to Satan as the "enemy of our human nature" (*SE* 136). The enemy wants to dehumanize and devalue us. In contrast, Jesus empowers us to embrace our humanity in all of its beautiful complexity. The more we express our humanity in loving, healing, forgiving, serving, and rejoicing, the more our divinity or holiness is revealed.

No definition or doctrine fully captures who Jesus Christ is. We are left with an alluring Mystery. Our deepening desire to know, love, and serve Jesus Christ draws us into this mystery of God becoming human for us.

The Gospel writers, living after the Resurrection and experiencing the Spirit alive in the church, present compelling portraits of this divine mystery. Contemplate the following stories from Scripture. Remember to include a colloquy in your prayer.

✝ PRAYER FOR THE WEEK

I pray for the following grace: to know Jesus more intimately, to love him more intensely, and to follow him more closely.

DAY 1

Read Matthew 14:22–33 (Jesus walks on water). Notice Peter's humanity: he expresses bold desires to do great things with Jesus, yet he also experiences real doubt. Listen to Jesus say to him and us: do not be afraid. Imagine yourself in the scene: How do you respond to Jesus' invitation?

DAY 2

Read Luke 9:18–36 (Peter's profession of faith and Jesus' transfiguration). How do you respond to Jesus' question: "Who do you say that I am?" How do you feel when you hear Jesus invite his disciples to "take up their cross"? What is it like to join the disciples on the holy mountain?

DAY 3

Read John 11:1–44 (Jesus raises Lazarus from the tomb). Notice Jesus' humanity in how he responds to the death of his dear friend and his divinity in raising him from the dead. Try to put yourself in the scene.

DAY 4

Repetition of one of the Scripture passages from days 1–3.

DAY 5

Read Luke 7:11–17 (Jesus raises widow's son). Notice again Jesus' human compassion and his marvelous deeds.

DAY 6

Read John 14:1–14 ("Do not let your hearts be troubled. Believe in God, believe also in me"). Let these words of Jesus at the Last Supper rest in you. What part of this discourse most connects with you?

DAY 7

Repetition of one of the Scripture passages from day 5 or 6.

St. Ignatius's Prayer for Generosity

Lord Jesus, teach me to be generous.
Teach me to serve you as you deserve,
To give and not to count the cost,
To fight and not to heed the wounds,
To toil and not to seek for rest,
To labor and not to seek reward,
Except that of knowing that I do your will.
Amen.

The Election: *Spiritual Exercises* 169–89

IGNATIUS INTENDED THE EXERCISES TO help people make important decisions. Ignatius offers us counsel in the part of the Exercises known as "the Election." He mentions in particular the choice of getting married or entering religious life. In addition to these decisions, the Exercises have helped people make a wide array of other choices about career, family, relationships, and lifestyle. For some, a particular decision may not be at issue. Instead, they may want simply to deepen their identity in Christ, a heartfelt commitment that will influence how they live after the retreat.

The Election does not apply to basic decisions between right and wrong; a person making the Exercises has already chosen to follow the way of Christ. Rather, the Election applies to noble commitments and choices between two or more *good* options.

The Election is made well into the retreat after much groundwork has been laid. Our prayer thus far has disposed us to make better decisions and choose Christ-like values. Putting the Principle and Foundation into practice, we have tried to recenter our lives, fixing our desires and intentions on the praise, love, and service of God above all else. Practicing the art of discernment, we have grown in awareness of how the good spirit and evil spirit act on us. Praying through Scripture, we have asked to see, hear, think, feel, choose, and act as Jesus does.

All along the way, we have begged for indifference—that is, freedom from any disordered love that gets in the way of our hearing God's call and responding to it wholeheartedly. We have learned to recast the questions, "What should I do? What do I want?" and ask instead, "What is *God's* desire for me and our world? How can I better love and serve God and others? How is God inviting me to a more meaningful, more joyful life?" Our myopic vision is thus transformed into the vision of God our Creator gazing upon the world in need and the vision of Jesus, sent to save us in our need.

We do not rush to answer these questions. We wait on God. Before we focus on the specifics of our calling, we turn our attention to the One who calls us. We spend weeks of the Exercises first getting to know the God who calls us, the One who creates, loves, forgives, and emboldens us, the God revealed most fully in Jesus Christ. The Exercises are built on the foundation that God communicates with us uniquely and personally and that we can come to know God by praying over Scripture, engaging the tradition and sacraments of the church, and relying on our intellect and imagination. We seek God in creation, in other people, and in the deepest desires of our heart. Sometimes we find God in very dramatic ways, but often it is in the most ordinary stuff of daily life that God reveals what God wants for us.

Traditionally, the church speaks of "finding" or "doing" the will of God. Such expressions recognize that God is our creator and that God's wisdom surpasses our own. The will of God, however, is not simply something imposed on us from the outside. Because we are created in the image of God, God is present to us at the deepest core of our being. We thus can discern the will of God in *our* deepest desires; this is Ignatius's novel insight. The Exercises help us sort through superficial and fleeting desires and tap into deep, holy longings. God's desires for us and our deepest desires are, in the end, not opposed but are one and the same.

With sharper vision, greater freedom, and a more discerning heart, we are better prepared to make concrete choices and commitments. Ignatius describes three situations in which a decision (or an election) is made:

1. The first situation is a time of clarity. In circumstances dramatic or very ordinary, God shows us the course to follow with such decisiveness that we know with great confidence that we are following God's lead. During this time, we are unable to doubt the rightness of the choice (although doubt may come later). We thank God for such times of graced conviction.

2. The second situation lacks such clarity. We experience opposing movements of certainty and doubt, spiritual consolation and desolation, strength and weakness. Such fluctuations are understandable because times of election are often moments of personal conversion, which we can both long for and resist. Here we apply the rules for the discernment of spirits to make a choice. These are the rules that we have been gradually learning and practicing throughout the retreat. We want to choose or commit out of experiences of authentic spiritual consolation and avoid acting out of spiritual desolation. Rely on a trusted spiritual mentor to help you sift through these various interior movements.

3. In the third situation, we experience no strong movements one way or the other. We are tranquil. To make a choice in this situation, we use our reason, enlightened by faith and informed by freedom. We first pray for guidance of the Spirit, and we recall our primary intention to praise, love, and serve God in any decision we make. Then we make use of the following exercises to help us make a decision with greater confidence and clarity:

- Weigh the advantages and disadvantages of accepting a proposed course of action and the pros and cons of rejecting it.
- Consider what advice you would give someone else considering the same choice.

- Imagine that you are on your deathbed, a perspective intended to give freedom and clarity to your decision. From the viewpoint of death, which puts everything else in perspective, consider which choice you would want to have made.

- Imagine standing in judgment before Christ when your life has ended and talking with him about the decision you made. From that viewpoint, consider which choice you would want to have made.

You can also try walking around for a day as if you made a certain decision, to see how it feels.

After making a decision, Ignatius insists that we pray for **confirmation** of the decision. There is no set time for doing so; we cannot rush grace. Confirmation may come in the next weeks of the retreat, as we deepen our commitment to Christ in his passion, death, and resurrection.

Once you offer the decision to God, look for signs of confirmation:

- Do you experience spiritual consolation (such as peace of mind and heart or a deeper desire to be with Christ) when considering the commitment or choice?

- Does your Spirit-guided reason lead you to the same conclusion? Does it give you new insight that increases your confidence in the choice?

- Has nothing come up in your prayer or thought that causes you to seriously question the decision?

Do not act if you are experiencing undue anxiety, confusion, or sadness.

Making an election, as with discernment of spirits, is more an art than a science. It takes practice. Choosing between two or more good options is difficult. Ignatius's rules for discernment and the methods of election can help us make decisions that lead to greater faith, hope, and love. In a culture that often runs from commitment and puts off decisions, we pray for wisdom, prudence, and courage in making choices. Although it is wise to take time to make a good decision, we should not delay decisions so much that we miss opportunities for growth. God will be with us, whatever course we take.

In the end, we make a decision in hope. If we made a good discernment and receive confirmation, then we can trust that this is the way that God asks us to use our freedom here and now. Something may happen in the future that requires us to make another discernment, but such events should not undermine our confidence in the initial discernment.

Once a choice is made, there are no guarantees that we will be successful (as the cross teaches us) or actually be able to do what we want (Ignatius was convinced that he was to spend his life in the Holy Land, but on his first try he was ordered to leave, and later, with his companions, he was not able to find safe passage there). We do our best to follow God's lead, and then we trust that God is with us in our decision making and will lead us where we need to go, even if by a circuitous route.

For Further Reflection

As we've seen, the Election can be an exercise in determining what your vocation in life is. Frederick Buechner, a popular theologian, writer, and Presbyterian minister, offers one of the most quoted definitions of vocation: "The place God calls you to is where your deep gladness and the world's deep hunger meet."

Similarly, Rev. Michael Himes of Boston College distills discernment about vocation to the following three questions: What gives me joy? Am I good at it? Does the world need it? This kind of discernment requires us to dig deep inside us, to be honest about our gifts and limitations, and to be generous with what we have.

The "Third Week"

†

*Being with Jesus in His Suffering and Savoring
the Grace of Compassion*

MY DAD LOVED KEY LIME PIE.

He was a Canadian by birth. He and my mom grew up and started their family in Montreal. But when my dad was in his early forties, he got an offer to work in the golf business in Palm Beach County, Florida, which in 1970 was another world compared to the cosmopolitan Montreal. Having lived his whole life in the snowy north, my dad bought three things when my mom, my brother, and my sister and I settled in sunny Florida: a house on the water (a smart move with the real estate boom coming), a Pontiac convertible, and fruit trees for our yard. A neighbor helped him plant a grapefruit tree, an orange tree, and a key lime tree (banana trees and an avocado tree would come later).

Thirty years later, only the key lime tree remained; the others were lost to disease or hurricanes. In his midseventies, my dad was diagnosed with Parkinson's disease. The disease progressed slowly; Dad stayed alert, remained fairly mobile, and was able to eat basically what he wanted to. But after he turned eighty, the decline became more rapid. He needed help bathing, exercising, and eventually eating. He had trouble talking at any length.

At the time, I was studying theology up in Boston, during my final years of preparation for ordination. On one of my visits home, I was driving my dad around to nowhere in particular, and out of the blue, he asked me, "So what are they teaching you up there?" I talked generally about some of my current courses in Scripture, moral theology, and the sacraments.

A long pause followed. "What do they teach you about what happens when you die?" he asked. Caught off guard, I stammered out an inarticulate response about hope and resurrection, a reply that was truthful but ethereal and not very grounded in Dad's present reality. If anyone else had asked the question, my response would have been far more smooth and pastoral; had I been preaching, the delivery would have been eloquent. But that day, I really wasn't present to my dad. I did not want to face the fact that he was going to die soon, so I dodged the question. Since then, I have so often replayed the conversation in my head and come up with a multitude of far more attentive responses for my father.

Just a month after being ordained a deacon, a ceremony my dad was not able to attend, I flew home for Thanksgiving. My brother and sister were out of state, spending some time with their families and in-laws. So it was just Mom, Dad, and me. With all the care my dad needed, Mom didn't have the energy to do elaborate cooking, so we ordered in a delicious meal. We set up the table for a traditional Thanksgiving dinner and placed my dad at his typical place at the head of our more formal dining table.

It was a bad day for him. He couldn't eat any of the turkey, stuffing, or mashed potatoes because he was unable to swallow well. But he kept eyeing the key lime pie. So we propped him up straight and I fed my father a spoonful of key lime pie. His face lit up. Unable to really talk, he nodded at me. I was able to manage a couple more spoonfuls before he couldn't digest anymore. The key lime pie would be his last solid food. The next day, we arranged for hospice care in my parents' home.

We didn't know how long it would be before Dad died. I returned to Boston to finish my exams quickly, then headed back home. I'd learned a lot of great theology in my Jesuit formation, but as Dad was dying, he silently schooled me in the art of presence. Unable to talk and slipping in and out of consciousness, he asked only that I be with him. My mother, brother, sister, and I took turns sitting at his bedside. It felt weird at first. I would just talk and hope something registered. Then I realized that words were not always necessary. I held his hand, gave him a sip of water, or moistened his face with a damp towel.

Toward the end, I developed the habit of praying with my dad at night. Throughout his life, he'd said his prayers on his knees before bed, a mode of praying I once dismissed as quaint but have returned to in my middle adulthood. So I would say the Our Father and Hail Mary out loud, hoping he could hear me. Sometimes I saw his lips move a little, as the first prayers he learned resonated deep within him. A few days before Christmas, Fr. O'Shea, our kind and generous parish priest for more than twenty years, came over, and we gathered around my father's bedside for the anointing of the sick. He died two days before Christmas.

In the **Third Week** of the Exercises, we journey with Jesus through his passion. In this part of the Exercises, we carry with us our own "passions," our personal experiences of suffering and death. The grace we pray for is simply to be with the Lord as he enters his suffering and death. During the Second Week, we were, seemingly, much more active. We were with the Lord in the midst of his very active ministry of healing, preaching, teaching, meeting, and comforting all sorts of people. We joined him on mission with growing zeal and fervor as God stirred within us noble desires for service.

In this phase of the Exercises, we accompany Jesus into the mystery of human suffering. Our prayer may become more still and quiet as a result. We don't need to make any big promises or figure out answers to timeless existential questions about the meaning of suffering. We just need to be present to Jesus and continue to have our hearts schooled about what compassion is all about. In this school of the heart, the cross becomes an extension of Jesus' ministry of loving presence, a love that is with us to the very end.

A few months before Dad died, I joined a group of Jesuits and lay students on a pilgrimage to El Salvador for the commemoration of the twenty-fifth anniversary of Archbishop Óscar Romero's death. Animated by the gospel of Jesus Christ and his commitment to the poor, Romero was a tireless advocate for peace and human rights in a country riddled with civil strife and mired in vast inequality between rich and poor. While saying Mass, Romero was assassinated by a militant aligned with the ruling party. On the anniversary visit, we spent some time at the University of Central America in San Salvador, which the Jesuits sponsor. Throughout the decadelong civil war that would claim more than seventy thousand lives, the Jesuits at the UCA, like Romero, called for social reforms and peace talks. They and their colleagues were passionate voices for the voiceless and faithful defenders of the victimized. In the middle of the night on November 16, 1989, a government-backed militia broke into the Jesuit residence at the UCA and executed six Jesuits along with their cook and her daughter.

Just as my father taught me about presence on a personal level, the words and example of Romero and the Jesuits of the UCA enlighten me about what presence means on a social level. If we take the gospel to heart—as we do during the Exercises—then we must stand with the poor and marginalized, not because God loves them more than the rich and well connected but simply because their needs are greater. The gospel demands such a stance because Jesus, a friend of rich and poor alike, always responded with compassion to those most in need. So as we walk through this week, we consider not only those whose suffering we know very personally but also those people in our community and world who live on the margins—the stepped on and stepped over, the left out and left behind. We choose to make our stand with them and do what we can to help them down from their crosses.

Such a "standing with" or "being with" expresses our solidarity with people who suffer. This is a prophetic moment in the Exercises, for in a world so divided, we proclaim that we belong to one another. No matter where we live or what we look like, whether or not we are related by blood, nationality, religion, or ethnicity, we say that we are accountable for one another; I'm accountable for my father and for the crucified peoples of our world because we are all children of God, who is our common origin and our end.

For Further Reflection

Lord, make me an instrument of your peace.
Where there is hatred, let me sow love;
where there is injury, pardon;
where there is doubt, faith;
where there is despair, hope;
where there is darkness, light;
and where there is sadness, joy.

O Divine Master, grant that I may not so much seek
to be consoled as to console,
to be understood as to understand,
to be loved as to love.
For it is in giving that we receive;
it is in pardoning that we are pardoned;
and it is in dying that we are born to eternal life.
Amen.

This prayer is often attributed to St. Francis of Assisi (1181–1226), but according to the official Vatican newspaper, *L'Osservatore Romano*, the prayer dates only to 1912. In 1916, as a world war raged, Pope Benedict XV directed the newspaper to publish the prayer more widely. After the war, the prayer began to appear on the backs of holy cards devoted to St. Francis. Like Ignatius of Loyola, Francis aspired to serve as a knight and enjoy a comfortable life. Whereas Ignatius's conversion began after he was hit by a cannonball during battle, Francis's life changed when he encountered a leper. He left his family home and served the poor and marginalized, in whom he saw Christ crucified. Other men and women were attracted to Francis's devotion and simple lifestyle. Francis was canonized just two years after his death, a sign of his manifest holiness. The Franciscan movement of religious and lay men and women continues to thrive today.

Week of Prayer #23:
The Road to Calvary

We enter the third phase or movement of the Spiritual Exercises. In the **Third Week**, we pray through the passion of Christ. In the Second Week, we asked for the grace to know Jesus more intimately, to love him more dearly, and to follow him more closely. This love leads us to be with Jesus in his suffering. Such is our natural response when someone we love is hurting or enduring hardship. We just want to stay with them, to be present to them, even when words fail and we are powerless to end their suffering.

The grace we seek in accompanying Christ through his suffering is compassion. We reflect not merely on the physical pain he endured but also on the emotional, interior suffering of a person who is misunderstood, isolated, rejected, and alone.

In the Third Week, then, we focus on being with Jesus and less on all the "doing" of the Second Week, where we accompanied Jesus in his active ministry. A certain stillness pervades the Third Week. We keep our eyes clearly fixed on Jesus and avoid any intense self-examination or weighing of values, as we have done in prior weeks. In doing so, we become more like the One we walk with to Calvary: more loving, more faithful, more generous, and more compassionate.

The colloquy is very important in the Third Week. It should flow naturally in your prayer. We speak to Jesus as a friend would speak to a friend (*SE* 54). We speak words of sorrow, confusion, compassion, regret, fear, anticipation—whatever moves us. Or perhaps we are present to him without words. The comfortable silence shared between friends can speak volumes.

✝ Prayer for the Week

"I ask for what I desire. Here it will be to ask for sorrow, regret, and confusion, because the Lord is going to his Passion for my sins" (*SE* 193).

Day 1
Read Matthew 21:1–11 (Jesus' entry into Jerusalem).

Day 2
Read Matthew 26:17–30 (Last Supper).

Day 3
Repetition.

Day 4
Read John 13:1–17 (washing of feet at the Last Supper).

Day 5
Read Matthew 26:36–46 or Luke 22:39–46 (agony in the garden).

Day 6
Repetition

Day 7
Savor the graces of the week.

For Further Reflection

There are truths that can be discovered only through suffering or from the critical vantage point of extreme situations.

—Fr. Ignacio Martín-Baró, SJ

Martín-Baró was a tireless advocate for social justice, killed at the University of Central America in El Salvador, November 16, 1989.

Rules for Discernment of Spirits: Distinguishing between Authentic and False Spiritual Consolation

As WE MOVE ALONG THE spiritual journey, we get better at noticing the spirits that operate on our souls. We understand how to respond to the obvious temptations, seductions, and deceits of the evil spirit. We become better at naming spiritual desolation and acting against it. We learn to run with the movements of the good spirit in times of consolation.

As our faith life deepens, however, we must be careful not to run too fast, because the enemy may change its tactics. The more we progress in the spiritual life, the more subtle and wily the evil spirit must become to achieve its destructive ends. In particular, the enemy may use consolation for its own purposes. That is, the enemy may come to us under the guise of consolation. Quietly and almost imperceptibly, the enemy may distract us with good feelings or undermine an experience of consolation to cause spiritual harm.

Ignatius explains:

> Both the good angel and the evil angel are able to cause consolation in the soul, but for their contrary purposes. The good angel acts for the progress of the soul, that it may grow and rise from what is good to what is better. The evil angel works for the

contrary purpose, that is, to entice the soul to his
own damnable intention and malice. (*SE* 331)

If both the good spirit and the evil spirit can cause or use spiritual consolation, then we must carefully discern the consolation we experience. How can we tell whether consolation is from God or from the enemy?

Ignatius first answers that there are times when we are absolutely convinced that the consolation is of God. He calls this experience "consolation without a preceding cause":

> It is the prerogative of the Creator alone to enter the
> soul, depart from it, and cause a motion in it which
> draws the whole person into love of His Divine
> Majesty. (*SE* 330)

In other words, there are times when we are simply bowled over by grace, whether we are doing something explicitly religious (like praying) or not (like washing dishes). We are undeniably caught up in a Love greater than ourselves. We experience this kind of consolation almost as a complete surprise, for it is not caused by anything we have done or thought or intended. In such moments, we simply give thanks and revel in the grace.

It is more often the case that some thought, memory, experience, or encounter triggers consolation. When that happens, we must discern carefully what has caused the consolation:

> It is characteristic of the evil angel, who takes on the
> appearance of an angel of light, to enter by going
> along the same way as the devout soul and then to
> exit by his own way with success for himself. That is,
> he brings good and holy thoughts attractive to such
> an upright soul and then strives little by little to get
> his own way, by enticing the soul over to his own
> hidden deceits and evil intentions. (*SE* 332)

For example, our prayer, worship, study, volunteer work, and experience in community may stir in us an enthusiastic response to Christ's call or a peaceful assurance that God is with us. These are typical signs of consolation. The evil spirit, however, can use such consolation for its own ends. Our zeal can turn into self-defeating overwork; confidence can devolve into arrogance and preoccupation with control; enthusiasm can become diffuse and scattered rather than focused and effective; sincere piety and religious conviction can turn into self-righteousness and closed-mindedness.

Note how clever the evil spirit is, coming to us under false pretenses, as an "angel of light," tempting people who are naturally attracted to apparently good things. We may not realize right away how far we have been led astray. Realizing that the enemy can use consolation against us is a first important step to getting back on track.

Week of Prayer #24:
The Arrest of Jesus

RECALL THAT IN THE CONTEMPLATION on the Incarnation, we heard the Trinity proclaim, "Let us work the redemption of the human race." We witnessed how God became one of us in Jesus of Nazareth, and we accompanied Jesus in his earthly life, watching divine generosity play out in the details of history. God's desire to save us from our inhumanity continues to unfold in Jesus' passion, which we contemplate during the Third Week.

Keep your eyes and heart fixed on Jesus. Use your imagination to place yourself in the scene if you like. Note in these meditations how much Jesus' opponents are concerned with self-seeking, face saving, and power tripping. Conversely, notice how Jesus refuses to play their games and instead remains true to who he is.

In your prayer, you may find yourself drawn to contemplate your own trials or the suffering of others, whether family, friends, or strangers. This is natural. However, the point is not to become absorbed in our own hardships but to embrace them as a source of compassion for the suffering of others.

As in the exercises of the First Week, when we considered ourselves as loved sinners, we personalize God's saving activity: Jesus endures suffering *for me*. This focus is not meant to induce guilt and to inflict needless pain on us. Rather, Jesus' offering is a sign of friendship with each of us, friendship that sacrifices for the other. It is this love that has deepened over the course of the Exercises.

✝ Prayer for the Week

"I ask for what I desire. Here it is what is proper for the Passion: sorrow with Christ in sorrow; a broken spirit with Christ so broken; tears; and interior suffering because of the great suffering which Christ endured for me" (*SE* 203).

Day 1
Read Matthew 26:47–56 (arrest of Jesus).

Day 2
Read John 18:12–27 (Jesus is brought before Annas and Caiaphas; Peter's denials).

Day 3
Read Matthew 26:57–75 (night session of the Sanhedrin; Peter's denials).

Day 4
Read Luke 22:66–71 (morning session of the Sanhedrin).

Day 5
Repetition.

Day 6
Read Isaiah 50:4–7.

Day 7
Savor the graces of the week.

For Further Reflection

It is often in challenging times that our vocation in life is tested and then, we hope, affirmed and deepened. As we've learned, our deepest passions and holy desires can reveal how God is calling us to live. Such depth of soul anchors us in rough waters. One of my favorite expressions of such soul-searching is by German poet, Rainer Maria Rilke (1875-1926). In his volume, *Letters to a Young Poet*, he writes:

You ask whether your verses are good. You ask me. You have asked others before. You send them to magazines. You compare them with other poems. . . . I beg you to give up all that. You are looking outward, and that above all you should not do now. Nobody can counsel and help you, nobody. There is only one single way. Go into yourself. Search for the reason that bids you write; find out whether it is spreading out its roots in the deepest places of your heart, acknowledge to yourself whether you would have to die if it were denied you to write. This above all—ask yourself in the stillest hour of your night: must I write? Delve into yourself for a deep answer. And if this should be affirmative, if you may meet this earnest question with a strong and simple "I must," then build your life according to this necessity; your life even into its most indifferent and slightest hour must be a sign of this urge and a testimony to it.

Rules for Discernment of Spirits: Discovering False Spiritual Consolation

WE CONTINUE TO REFLECT ON how the evil spirit can enter our lives under the guise of consolation. What begins as an experience of consolation ends—to our surprise—with spiritual desolation (such as disquiet, anxiety, fear, self-involvement, or bitterness). Or a course of thinking or acting may result in our sinning, hurting someone else, or missing an opportunity for grace:

> We should pay close attention to the whole train of our thoughts. If the beginning, middle, and end are all good and tend toward what is wholly good, it is a sign of the good angel. But if the train of the thoughts which a spirit causes ends up in something evil or diverting, or in something less good than what the soul was originally proposing to do; or further, if it weakens, disquiets, or disturbs the soul, by robbing it of the peace, tranquility, and quiet which it enjoyed earlier, all this is a clear sign that this is coming from the evil spirit, the enemy of our progress and eternal salvation. (*SE* 333)

Here, we notice how a course of thinking or acting led us to a dead end despite our best intentions. Although we cannot undo the past, we can always ask for forgiveness from God or others and seek the help we need to undo any damage. And by reflecting on the whole train of our connected thoughts or actions, we can learn from our mistakes and avoid such detours in the future.

How much better if we can notice how the enemy is roaming about *before* the damage is done! Ignatius addresses such graced awareness in another rule for discernment:

> When the enemy of human nature has been perceived and recognized by his serpent's tail and the evil end to which he is leading, it then becomes profitable for the person whom he has tempted in this way to examine the whole train of the good thoughts which the evil spirit brought to the soul; that is, how they began, and then how little by little the evil spirit endeavored to bring the soul down from the sweetness and spiritual joy in which it had been, and finally brought it to his own evil intention. The purpose is that through this experience, now recognized and noted, the soul may guard itself in the future against these characteristic snares. (*SE* 334)

The enemy works subtly, distracting us little by little and corrupting consolation. If we catch a glimpse of the tail of the serpent, then we should immediately pause and trace the course of our thoughts and actions *before* moving ahead. For example, if I find myself irritable, exhausted, and overworked while working on some noble project I used to love, I should pause to discern how I arrived at this miserable place. This is a difficult but graced awareness. I should be thankful that I caught myself before more harm was done.

The bottom line is that we should judge the spirit by its fruits: *where did it lead us?* Discernment takes time and practice. A daily Examen is invaluable to integrating discernment with our daily thoughts and actions, as is talking with a trusted and wise spiritual guide. With time, effort, good counsel, and the grace of God, we can better discern the spirits and in doing so harness authentic consolations, uncover false consolations, and resist desolations.

WEEK OF PRAYER #25: THE SUFFERING AND DEATH OF JESUS

IN THE THIRD WEEK OF the Exercises, Ignatius invites us to consider how Jesus' divinity "hides itself" (*SE* 196). We must not easily explain away the suffering we encounter. Jesus is not merely playacting his way through a passion play. We must take Jesus' humanity seriously enough to realize just how much he loves us. He remains faithful to his Father and the mission of the kingdom and accepts the very real consequences of that faithful obedience, which he does out of great love.

As you pray through the Passion and ask for the grace of compassion, consider how you are called to be more compassionate in the particulars of your own life. Ask: *What invisible crosses do people bear? How can I help carry them? Who helps carry my own burdens? Who are the crucified peoples of our world today?*

We experience various "dyings," losses of different kinds, and we must mourn them: the death of a loved one, the loss of a relationship, the change of a career or living situation, a physical infirmity or limitation. We unite these dyings with the suffering of Christ, knowing that God redeems all. Recall a line from the contemporary version of the *Anima Christi*: "On each of my dyings, shed your light and your love." This week, conclude each prayer time with the *Anima Christi* (pp. 41–42).

✝ Prayer for the Week

"I ask for what I desire. Here it is what is proper for the Passion: sorrow with Christ in sorrow; a broken spirit with Christ so broken; tears; and interior suffering because of the great suffering which Christ endured for me" (*SE* 203).

Day 1
Read Luke 23:1–25 (the trial before Pilate and Herod).

Day 2
Read Matthew 27:26–31 (the crowning with thorns).

Day 3
Read Luke 23:26–32 (the way of the cross).

Day 4
Read Luke 23:33–49 (the Crucifixion). Notice how Jesus, even in his suffering, is still reaching out to console the lost sheep, in this case the "good thief."

Day 5
Repetition.

Day 6
Read Isaiah 52:13–53:12.

Day 7
Read John 10:1–18 (Jesus, the Good Shepherd).

Colloquy before Christ Crucified:
Contemporary Translation

I put myself before Jesus Christ our Lord, present before me on the cross.

I talk to him about how he creates because he loves and then he is born one like us out of love, so emptying himself as to pass from eternal life to death here in time, even death on a cross. By his response of love for God his Father, he dies for my sins.

I look to myself and ask—just letting the questions penetrate my being:

In the past, what response have I made to Christ?
How do I respond to Christ now?
What response should I make to Christ?

As I look upon Jesus as he hangs upon the cross, I ponder whatever God may bring to my attention. (*SE* 53)

We prayed this colloquy during the First Week of the Exercises. As we come to this part of the retreat, contemplating the passion of our Lord, keep the colloquy close to your heart. The contemporary translation is by David L. Fleming, in *Draw Me into Your Friendship: The Spiritual Exercises—A Literal Translation and a Contemporary Reading*.

WEEK OF PRAYER #26: THE PASCHAL MYSTERY

THE PASCHAL MYSTERY REFERS TO the unfolding of God's plan of salvation in Christ's passion, death, and resurrection. Although we should not run from the sadness and confusion of the Passion, we also should not induce amnesia, forgetting that the glory of Easter morning follows the darkness of Good Friday. The birth, life, death, and resurrection of Christ are different movements of the same symphony of God's extravagant love for us:

> For God so loved the world that he gave his only Son, so that everyone who believes in him may not perish but may have eternal life. (John 3:16)

When viewed through Easter eyes, the cross no longer stands as a sign of defeat but of God's victory over everything opposed to the kingdom of God. Jesus took on the forces of violence and death—and won!

Questions may stir in us these weeks: *Why did Jesus have to die for us? How does Jesus' death atone for our sins? How does my own suffering unite with Jesus' suffering on the cross?* These are all good questions, but they are probably best left for after the retreat so that they don't become distractions during these weeks of prayer.

✝ Prayer for the Week

"I ask for what I desire. Here it is what is proper for the Passion: sorrow with Christ in sorrow; a broken spirit with Christ so broken; tears; and interior suffering because of the great suffering which Christ endured for me" (*SE* 203).

Day 1

Pray the first half of the Passion, Mark 14:12–72. Pray it as a whole or linger over different parts. Use the Application of the Five Senses (p. 140) to deepen and simplify your prayer.

Day 2

Pray the second half of the Passion, Mark 15:1–47.

Day 3

Read Luke 23:50–56 (Jesus is laid in the tomb). In this Holy Saturday moment, we wait in stillness, loss, and longing. Try to find stillness of soul this week.

Day 4

Read Philippians 2:1–11 (one of the most ancient hymns to Jesus Christ in the Bible).

Day 5

Read 2 Corinthians 4:7–18 (we carry in us the life and death of Jesus).

Day 6

Read Psalm 116 ("You have delivered my soul from death").

Day 7

Savor the graces of the week.

For Further Reflection

In the shadow of death
may we not look back to the past,
but seek in utter darkness the dawn of God.

Lord, enfold me in the depths of your heart;
and there hold me,
refine, purge, and set me on fire,
raise me aloft,
until my own self knows utter annihilation.

—Pierre Teilhard de Chardin, SJ

The "Fourth Week"

✝

*Experiencing the Joy and Sharing the
Consolation of the Risen Lord*

IN THE FOURTH WEEK OF the Spiritual Exercises, we encounter the risen Lord as he consoles his friends and disciples, who were once scared, confused, and despairing. Accompanying the One we have walked with all along, we savor the distinctive grace of this final movement of the Exercises: **joy**. This Easter joy eludes simple description, just as love has eluded description by countless poets, songwriters, and lovers. From our experience, we know that joy is more than just happiness, which can come and go and sometimes be induced. Joy is something deeper than mere emotion. A sure sign of God's presence, joy is a gift from God, freely given and often unexpected. We can experience joy in the company of others or in the beauty of nature. We can also experience joy in our work when *who we are* and *what we do* are in synch.

Perhaps the best way to understand joy is to see it in action. There are some typically joyful moments, very human moments, that I am privileged to share in as a priest: births and baptisms, weddings and anniversaries, community celebrations and the sacrament of reconciliation. Let me share two stories from my ministry when, to borrow from the title of C. S. Lewis's classic book, I was "surprised by joy."

While studying theology in Boston, I helped out on weekends at a large middle-class, suburban parish. The people of St. Raphael's welcomed me with open arms. On one of my first Sundays there, Fr. Kevin, the pastor, assigned me to preach the family Mass, where there would be lots of children. The Gospel of the day had to do with faith. I knew I had to do something eye catching to get the children's attention and communicate a basic point about the meaning of faith: why we believe what we do not see.

As I began the homily, I showed the packed church a brown-paper lunch bag, in which I had put some candy before Mass began. Without showing them the candy inside, I told them that there was candy in the bag. I invited children to come forward, sit around the altar, and answer some questions from me about why they believe that there is candy in the bag even though they cannot see any of it. Their reward for so bravely coming forward would be some of the candy (to be eaten after Mass, of course). I expected that only a few courageous children would come forward in front of such a big crowd, but the lure of candy overcame any reluctance. More than thirty children converged on the altar at once! It was a lively homily to say the least. Their parents loved it. But at the conclusion, I was embarrassed to admit that I did not have enough candy for everyone, so I promised that I would come back next week with an ample supply.

Toward the end of Mass, I noticed some commotion in the back of the church. Before the concluding blessing, the head usher got my attention to wait. He and a few others then came forward with collection baskets full of candy. Turns out that when some parents noticed my predicament during the homily, they ran across the street to the drugstore and bought bags of candy, enough for all of the children in the church. Deeply moved and speechless, I recovered with a joke about having witnessed a modern-day version of multiplication of loaves and fishes. I left that morning feeling very much at home at the parish and filled with such unexpected joy in the community's welcome and generosity to me and to one another.

A few years later, I was working at Georgetown University, teaching and serving as director of Campus Ministry. Over spring break one year, I took a group of students down to El Salvador on a faith-based immersion trip. After a few days in the capital, we spent three days in a small village a two-hour bus ride away. Over the years, Georgetown had built a relationship with the people of the village, many of whom had settled there after the civil war ended in the early 1990s. Each of the hundred families in the village had a story to tell about someone killed or missing during the war. Their mode of living was very simple. Most bathrooms and showers were outside their simple, concrete houses. The streets were not paved, and electricity was limited. The people were incredibly generous with what they had, inviting us into their homes to sleep and feeding us homemade meals.

Over breakfast one morning I learned from one of the village leaders that a priest came to the village only once a month. As in many rural towns in Latin America, lay men and women are the heart of the church, organizing religious education and communion services. Somewhat tentatively, I offered to say Mass, my first in Spanish. Word spread through the village that there would be Mass that night at seven o'clock in the chapel, which was next to the school on the main road leading into the town.

As the day wore on, I became more and more nervous. I feverishly studied the small leaflet that contained the readings and the parts of the Mass in Spanish. At seven o'clock only a few people beyond our group of twelve from Georgetown were in the chapel, but within fifteen minutes, the place was packed. Dogs and cats wandered in and out. A young man brought a guitar (almost a necessity for any Mass in Latin America). A teenage girl volunteered as the altar server. She was my lifeline, prompting me with the right words as I made my way through the Mass in an unfamiliar tongue.

I was most nervous about the homily because I would be speaking in Spanish without notes. Walking to the center aisle, I spoke a few words about what solidarity meant. I then invited a couple of our students from Georgetown to say a few words about how they had experienced community during their visit. This prompted several of our hosts to reflect on the Gospel. More people joined in. What followed was an amazing, graced dialogue about how faith crossed cultures and the love of God and neighbor brought very different people together as a family.

As I stepped back and soaked it all in, I realized how the Mass was so much greater than me getting the words right. The Holy Spirit was stirring. This was made all the more clear during the sign of peace that followed the Eucharistic Prayer. It seemed everyone greeted or hugged everyone else. It lasted a long while, which made communion even more meaningful. Just as in that suburban parish in Boston, I was surprised by joy, and for that evening, I knew I wanted to be nowhere else in the world.

The joy we experience in our "ordinary" lives puts us in touch with this divine embrace. These two experiences took place in explicitly religious settings, but we can taste joy in any part of our lives and in some unexpected places. I found joy (or joy found me) at Fenway Park, and it had nothing to do with the Red Sox winning.

As I wrote earlier, my father died just before Christmas. After the funeral rites, I headed back to Boston to finish my theology studies, anticipating ordination in June. Each person's grieving is unique. In the months after his death, I felt his loss deeply, without much consolation. In May, my brother Andy visited me in Boston and brought me to a Red Sox game. My dad was a baseball player in his youth, and we boys went to many baseball games when we were growing up (although we inherited none of our dad's natural athletic ability). There was a moment early in the game when the sun was setting behind us, on a clear blue, warm spring evening. Long shadows crossed the perfectly green field. The atmosphere was electric in the park, as the new season meant summer was near and life's possibilities were endless. And I was with my brother. In unison, we raised our cold beers in a toast to our father: "He would have loved this," we said, practically in unison. "To Dad." In that moment between brothers, on that hallowed ground, I felt Dad's presence with us in a very real way.

We can find joy amid the most challenging of circumstances. The first time I really felt at home in India—after my initial struggles and hardship—was playing soccer with the kids in the cow pasture behind the Nirmala Hospital compound. It was the closest thing they had to a field. In the middle of our game, the monsoon rains came, but we just kept playing, laughing, sliding, and falling into the mud (and whatever else the cows left us!). Inexplicably, at that moment, I knew that this small patch of earth in India was where I was meant to be.

Such encounters with joy stir up hope in us. And this hope, to quote the English poet Alexander Pope, "springs eternal in the human breast." When I left the immigration detention center outside Los Angeles, one of the resident artists gave me a gift, which still adorns my bedroom: a rose made out of folded and twisted toilet paper, with the leaves tinted green and the flower red with the dye of M&M candies diluted in water. In the garden where the Jesuits in San Salvador were murdered, red roses now bloom, planted by the husband and father of the two women who were murdered alongside the Jesuits. These roses reveal to me the resilience of hope. The Fourth Week reminds us that death, despair, violence, and sadness will not have the last word: joy does. Walking with the risen Lord, we appreciate how Easter is happening all the time, with joy surprising us everywhere.

Week of Prayer #27: The Resurrection of Jesus Christ

WE NOW ENTER INTO THE last movement or "week" of the retreat. In the Third Week, we shared in Christ's sorrow and anguish. Now, in the **Fourth Week**, we ask to share in the joy and peace of the risen Christ. This joy, like any grace we pray for, is a gift from God; we cannot earn or force it. We simply try to be open to receiving Easter joy by contemplating Christ as he shares the joy of the Resurrection with others.

Easter joy is rooted in each person's relationship with Christ, cultivated over a lifetime and deepened through the Exercises and other spiritual practices. Joy comes as we grow in faith, hope, and love. The author of 1 Peter 1:8–9 describes an experience akin to living in the Fourth Week:

> Although you have not seen him, you love him; and even though you do not see him now, you believe in him and rejoice with an indescribable and glorious joy, for you are receiving the outcome of your faith, the salvation of your souls.

We are not contemplating the actual resurrection event, which is a mystery, beyond time and space. *Resurrection* refers to the event of God's transformation of life, making all things new, as in a new creation. Resurrection is a conquering of sin and death, once and for all. Instead of being distracted by the mechanics of the Resurrection or what a resurrected body looks like, we simply contemplate the risen Christ consoling others. We notice how his friends both recognize and fail to recognize the One they have followed and loved. We marvel at how Jesus in the resurrected life—where his divinity is no longer hidden—does very human things: eating, talking, consoling, teaching, and enjoying the company of others. As with the mystery of the Incarnation, we see in the Resurrection how our divinity and humanity are not opposed but are an integral part of each other.

✝ Prayer for the Week

"I ask for what I desire. Here it will be to ask for the grace to be glad and to rejoice intensely because of the great glory and joy of Christ our Lord" (*SE* 221).

Day 1

Read John 20:1–10 (the disciples find the empty tomb). Imagine finding the empty tomb with the disciples.

Day 2

The following contemplation is not found in the Scriptures but comes from Ignatius's own imagination. Given the central role that Mary played in Jesus' life, Ignatius thinks it only reasonable that the first person to whom Christ appeared was his mother. So imagine the risen Christ appearing to Mary. Imagine the details of the room where they meet. Imagine how each is so excited and joy filled upon their reunion. Imagine the words and embraces they exchange. See how Christ consoles her (*SE* 218–225).

Day 3

Repetition.

Day 4

Read John 20:11–18 (Jesus appears to Mary Magdalene). Notice how Mary at first does not recognize Jesus until he lovingly says her name. Imagine her confusion, her relief, her excitement, her joy! Hear and see how Jesus commissions her (and you).

Day 5

Read Matthew 28:1–10 (Jesus appears to the women at the tomb). Hear again from the angels and Jesus what you've heard often in the retreat: "Do not be afraid." Love casts out all fear. Joy remains.

Day 6

Repetition.

Day 7

Savor the graces of the week. Read 2 Corinthians 1:3–7 ("the God of all consolation").

For Further Reflection

We will never win the Olympics of humanity,
racing for perfection,
but we can walk together in hope,
celebrating that we are loved in our brokenness:
helping each other,
growing in trust,
living in thanksgiving,
learning to forgive,
opening up to others and welcoming them,
and striving to bring peace and hope to the world.

—JEAN VANIER

JEAN VANIER is founder of L'Arche and cofounder of Faith and Light, intentional faith-based communities where persons with developmental disabilities and those without choose to live together. He still lives in the first L'Arche community in France but travels widely giving retreats and speeches. For more information, see the Web site of L'Arche USA (http://www.larcheusa.org).

Week of Prayer #28:
The Risen Life

IN THE CONTEMPLATIONS THAT FOLLOW, continue to reflect on the role of Christ as consoler. In your own life, look for signs of how God has consoled and continues to console you and the people around you. *Where do I find joy? Who or what gives me joy?*

We experience various "dyings," not just with the death of loved ones but also with the loss of friendships, changes in life-style or career, physical infirmity, children leaving home, and our own relocations from one city to another. Our God, however, is a God of life. The Resurrection reveals how God is always bringing life from death, hope from despair, love from hate, and light from darkness. So we celebrate the "risings" as well, such as reconciled or new friendships, unexpected opportunities, renewed vigor, and meaningful learning experiences that come from losses.

Notice how the risen Christ still bears the marks of the Crucifixion. This itself is a consoling image. Our hurts and limitations are part of who we are. In death, they are not wiped away but are redeemed. God takes us as we are and makes us whole again. A new creation is at work. God wastes nothing and redeems all.

✝ Prayer for the Week

"I ask for what I desire. Here it will be to ask for the grace to be glad and to rejoice intensely because of the great glory and joy of Christ our Lord" (*SE* 221).

Day 1

Read Luke 24:13–35 (Jesus appears to the disciples on the way to Emmaus). Notice again how Jesus' disciples do not recognize him at first. Notice too how Jesus just walks and listens to the disciples in their sadness and confusion. How has Jesus walked with you these weeks? How do the disciples—and how do you—recognize the risen Christ? How have you experienced your heart burning these weeks? What desires are stirring in your heart now?

Day 2

Read Luke 24:36–49 (Jesus appears to the apostles). Notice how the risen Christ greets his friends, and us, with the gift of peace. Where in your life do you wish for peace? In what situations can you give the gift of peace?

Day 3

Repetition.

Day 4

Read John 20:19–23 (Jesus appears to the disciples). Notice how Jesus meets the disciples amid their fears and gives them the comfort of the Spirit in such an intimate gesture. The Spirit liberates them from their fears and sends them out of their locked room to a world in need. What fears do you face? Where do you experience the comfort of the risen Christ? Are you experiencing a sense of mission at this point in your retreat?

Day 5

Read John 20:24–31 (Jesus appears to "doubting Thomas"). Notice how compassionately Jesus deals with doubts, which are a natural part of a faith journey. Periods of doubt and questioning can lead to a stronger, more deeply held faith. The key is to keep the conversation going with the Lord, as you have been doing throughout your retreat and as Thomas does with Jesus. Can you relate to Thomas's doubting? Can you say with him the great proclamation of faith that concludes this Gospel story: "My Lord and my God!"

Day 6

Read John 21:1–19 (Jesus appears to Peter and the disciples). Imagine yourself in this very dynamic scene. Can you feel the disciples' excitement and wonder and Peter's enthusiasm? Listen to the intimate dialogue between Jesus and Peter. Imagine Jesus saying the same to you. Notice the command that Jesus leaves Peter. How are you called to "feed" and "tend" to others?

Day 7

Repetition.

For Further Reflection

In the final analysis, talking about prayer doesn't matter; rather, only the words that we ourselves say to God. And one must say these words oneself.

Oh, they can be quiet, poor, and diffident. They can rise up to God's heaven like silver doves from a happy heart, or they can be the inaudible flowing of bitter tears. They can be great and sublime like thunder that crashes in the high mountains, or diffident like the shy confession of a first love.

If they only come from the heart. If they only might come from the heart. And if only the Spirit of God prays them together also. Then God hears them. Then he will forget none of these words. Then he will keep the words in his heart because one cannot forget the words of love.

And then he will listen to us patiently, even blissfully, an entire life long until we are through talking, until we have spoken out our entire life. And then he will say one single word of love, but he is this word itself. And then our heart will stop beating at this word. For eternity.

Don't we want to pray?

—KARL RAHNER, *THE NEED AND THE BLESSING OF PRAYER*

Week of Prayer #29: The Contemplation of the Love of God

THE FINAL CONTEMPLATION IN THE text of the Exercises, the **Contemplation of the Love of God** (*SE* 230–237), is the culmination of the weeks of prayer that precede it. In this contemplation, we draw on our experience of God's overwhelming love in the Exercises to inform and empower our lives going forward. From this vantage point, we see that the whole movement of the retreat has been rooted in and oriented toward love.

In the Principle and Foundation, we considered how we are created to love and serve God, relying on the goods of creation only to the extent that they help us love God and others. In the First Week, we came to see ourselves first as beloved creatures of God, and to know that God's love for us is not diminished by our sin and weakness. In the Second Week, we heard the call of Jesus and followed him throughout his ministry of love, mercy, and reconciliation. We have stood with the one who has loved us so totally, suffering with him in the Third Week and rejoicing with him in the triumph of the Fourth Week. In the process, something has happened to us. We are not the same as we were. Our eyes are different, and we see the world in light of God's love. Our hearts are different, too. They are aflame with generosity, freedom, and passion.

German poet Rainer Maria Rilke captures the movement of this Contemplation (indeed the whole Exercises) perfectly: "We are cradled close in your hands—and lavishly flung forth." We have answered the call to "come and see" (John 1:39), and at this point reach a critical juncture. Now we must take the love and grace that God has given us during this privileged time of retreat and incarnate it in our own lives.

In contemplating the love of God, we ask for the grace to love as God loves. To this end, Ignatius offers two critical insights:

1. "Love ought to manifest itself more by deeds than by words" (*SE* **230**). Love must be put into action; words are not enough. Having been schooled as disciples these many weeks, we must now *do* something. Ignatian spirituality is one of mission.

2. "Love consists in a mutual communication between the two persons" (*SE* **231**). Just as the love between two persons is marked by giving and receiving, the love we share with God enjoys a certain mutuality. God wants our friendship. God wants to be known by us. These divine desires are the source of our desire to know, love, and serve God.

In the contemplation that follows these observations, we first consider how God loves us into existence and sustains us in love. All is possible because God loves us first. This love by nature overflows into the world we inhabit and into every part of our lives. In this contemplation, we ask for the vision to "find God in all things." To use images crafted by Gerard Manley Hopkins, a nineteenth-century Jesuit poet, we want to notice how "the world is charged with the grandeur of God," and how "Christ plays in ten thousand places" and faces.

Attentive to God's presence everywhere and recognizing God's generosity to us, we naturally want to return the favor by praising, loving, and serving God and helping others. As the title of a poem by Richard Wilbur tells us, "Love Calls Us to the Things of This World." Nowhere is this clearer than in the life, death, and resurrection of Jesus Christ.

As we pray this contemplation, Ignatius suggests that we place ourselves in God's presence by imagining that we are "standing before God our Lord, and also before the angels and saints," who are praying for us (*SE* 232). You may want to add to that heavenly host loved ones who have died and people who have shown you what loving is all about.

✝ Prayer for the Week

"I ask for what I desire. Here it will be to ask for interior knowledge of all the great good I have received, in order that, stirred to profound gratitude, I may become able to love and serve the Divine Majesty in all things" (*SE* 233).

Day 1
The first point of the Contemplation: **thanking God for so many gifts.**

> I will call back into my memory the gifts I have received—my creation, redemption, and other gifts particular to myself. I will ponder with deep affection how much God our Lord has done for me, and how much he has given me of what he possesses, and consequently how he, the same Lord, desires to give me even his very self, in accordance with his divine design.
>
> Then I will reflect on myself, and consider what I on my part ought in all reason and justice to offer and give to the Divine Majesty, namely, all my possessions, and myself along with them. I will speak as one making an offering with deep affection, and say:
>
> *Take, lord, and receive all my liberty, my memory, my understanding, and all my will—all that I have and possess. You, Lord, have given all that to me. I now give it back to you, O Lord.*

All of it is yours. Dispose of it according to your will.
Give me love of yourself along with your grace, for
that is enough for me. (*SE* 234)

The Take, Lord, Receive prayer is an offering made in freedom. We have been praying for indifference throughout the retreat: to become free of disordered loves. Now we focus on why this freedom is necessary: we become free from excessive attachments so that we can love and serve God and others *more.* Basking in the love of God, we are empowered to love as God loves.

Day 2
Repetition of the first point of the Contemplation. If helpful in your prayer of thanksgiving, revisit Psalm 139 from earlier in the retreat or Psalm 138, a hymn of gratitude. In praying with the Take, Lord, Receive prayer, ask: *What are my particular gifts, talents, and other blessings that I want to offer for the service of God and others?*

Day 3
The second point of the contemplation: **finding God in all things, in all people, and in myself.**

> I will consider how God dwells in creatures; in the elements, giving them existence; in the plants, giving them life; in the animals, giving them sensation; in human beings, given them intelligence; and finally, how in this way he dwells also in myself, giving me existence, life, sensation, and intelligence; and even further, making me his temple, since I am created as a likeness and image of the Divine Majesty. Then once again I will reflect on myself, in the manner

described in the first point, or in any other way I
feel to be better. (*SE* 235)

Use your senses and imagination to find God in all things and
all people. Be attentive to the movements of grace within you.
Conclude with the Take, Lord, Receive prayer.

Day 4

Repetition of Day 3. With the eyes of faith, we realize the
infinite depth of reality. We begin to understand how much
of heaven is here on earth. God is with us. Ask: *How have I
encountered God dwelling in me, in others, and in creation?* Be
very concrete. You may consider praying outdoors in nature. If
helpful, revisit Psalm 104 from earlier in the retreat.

Day 5

The third point of the contemplation: **praising God who con-
stantly labors for me.**

I will consider how God labors and works for me
in all the creatures on the face of the earth; that
is, he acts in the manner of one who is laboring. For example, he is working in the heavens,
elements, plants, fruits, cattle, and all the rest—
giving them their existence, conserving them,
concurring with their vegetative and sensitive
activities. Then I will reflect on myself. (*SE* 236)

God is not static. God—revealed to us as Father, Son, and
Holy Spirit—is dynamic, alive, always stirring, and always
laboring to bring life to God's beloved creation. God is love
overflowing. In your prayer, consider the activity of God
in your life and your world. Marvel at how God creates in,
through, and with us. Can you see and hear God laboring

in the world around you? Can you appreciate how God has "labored" specifically in and through you? Can you recognize how the labor of others supports you in your living? Conclude with the Take, Lord, Receive prayer.

DAY 6
The fourth point of the contemplation: **praising God, who is the source of all goodness.**

> I will consider how all good things and gifts descend from above; for example, my limited power from the Supreme and Infinite Power above; and so of justice, goodness, piety, mercy, and so forth—just as the rays come down from the sun, or the rains from their source. Then I will finish by reflecting on myself. (*SE* 237)

Love sees clearly into the depths of reality. With your vision sharpened by the Exercises, try to see in all things—in all creation and all people—the reflection of God's very self. Recall specific occasions when you or someone else acted with justice, goodness, mercy, or another virtue. Appreciate how these actions were like "rays come down from the sun," who is God. Conclude with the Take, Lord, Receive prayer.

DAY 7
Savor the graces of the week. Let gratitude permeate your prayer. Gratitude is freeing, for it opens us up to give what we have so abundantly received. Grateful people are happy people. If helpful, revisit John 21:1–19 from last week. A trusted spiritual guide, Howard Gray, SJ, suggested this story to me as a recapitulation of the Contemplation of the Love of God because we meet the risen Christ, who gives the disciples an abundance of gifts, labors for them, and invites them into

friendship. He loves them concretely and asks Peter in particular to return that love in very concrete ways for the good of others.

For Further Reflection

Lord, You have made us for Yourself,
and our hearts are restless until they rest in You.

—St. Augustine, *Confessions*

The day will come when, after harnessing the space, the winds, the tides, gravitation, we shall harness for God the energies of love. And, on that day, for the second time in the history of the world, man will have discovered fire.

—Pierre Teilhard de Chardin, SJ,
Toward the Future

A Prayer by Rabindranath Tagore

Let Your love play upon my voice and rest on my silence.

Let it pass through my heart into all my movements.

Let Your love, like stars, shine in the darkness of my sleep
and dawn in my awakening.

Let it burn in the flame of my desires
and flow in all currents of my own love.

Let me carry Your love in my life
as a harp does its music,
and give it back to You at last with my life.

The Indian poet Rabindranath Tagore (1861–1941) was a friend
of Mahatma Gandhi. Tagore won the Nobel Prize in Literature
in 1913.

Week of Prayer #30: Life in the Spirit

JESUS SENDS US THE SPIRIT so that we can continue to grow in faith, hope, and love, and live out our mission as disciples today. The Spirit consoles, encourages, animates, enlivens, emboldens, and gives us work to do. In one sense, the Holy Spirit is a deeply personal gift, but like love, the Spirit is also shared. The Spirit of God forms us into one body, the church universal. A fruit of the Fourth Week, then, is our willingness and enthusiasm to commit ourselves to a person (Jesus Christ), a people (all of God's children), and a project (the kingdom of God).

The church has long celebrated certain gifts of the Holy Spirit. We recall them now as we reflect on how these gifts are concretely present: wisdom, understanding, right judgment, courage, knowledge, reverence, and wonder and awe in God's presence (see Isaiah 11:1–2).

✝ Prayer for the Week

I pray for the following grace: a deepening awareness of the presence, power, and movement of the Spirit in my life.

Day 1
Read John 14:16–31 (Jesus' promise to send the Holy Spirit).

Day 2

Read Matthew 28:1–10, 16–20 (the Resurrection and Ascension narrative).

Day 3

Read Acts 2:1–24; 37–47 (Pentecost; the first converts).

Day 4

Repetition.

Day 5

Read 2 Timothy 1:3–14 ("God did not give us a spirit of cowardice, but rather a spirit of power and of love and of self-discipline").

Day 6

Read Corinthians 12:4–27 (the Body of Christ).

Day 7

Repetition.

A Prayer by St. Teresa of Ávila

Christ has no body but yours.
No hands, no feet on earth but yours.
Yours are the eyes
with which He looks compassion on this world.
Yours are the feet
with which He walks to do good.
Yours are the hands
with which He blesses all the world.

Yours are the hands.
Yours are the feet.
Yours are the eyes.
You are His body.

Christ has no body now on earth but yours.

Week of Prayer #31:
Gathering the Graces

Over the weeks of the retreat, you have learned to follow the lead of the Spirit. With the aid of the Spirit, review the retreat now to discern the key graces you have experienced. Don't replay the retreat day by day or week by week. Instead, as you would do in the repetition of a prayer period, go back to what is most significant. Remember in gratitude God's generosity to you, and acknowledge your own generous cooperation with grace.

Review your journal. As you do, try to summarize in brief statements the most meaningful insights and movements of the retreat. Some questions to consider:

- How has my awareness of God's presence in my life grown or shifted?

- What ways of praying were most meaningful or challenging for me?

- How have I grown in knowledge and love of Christ?

- Where have I experienced greater interior freedom?

- Where is there still disorder or lack of interior freedom in my life?

- How do I most usually experience consolation and desolation?

- How do the good spirit and evil spirit usually operate in my life?

When answering these questions, be as concrete as you can. If helpful, you can organize your review by the four "weeks" of the *Exercises*. This taking stock will help you integrate the graces into daily life and remember them in the future, as benchmarks in your spiritual journey.

The Scripture suggestions for this week are intended to assist you in your gathering of the graces of the retreat. As always, rely on them as helpful.

Even as you conduct this spiritual inventory, acknowledge that no statement—no matter how artfully written—can capture adequately the mystery of God's laboring in your life. All statements about God end in an ellipsis of sorts, with more to come.

✝ Prayer for the Week

I pray for the following grace: a deepening awareness and gratitude for God's faithful presence in my life.

Day 1
Read Romans 8:14–27 (living in the Spirit).

Day 2
Read Romans 8:28–39 (a hymn to God's glory; nothing can separate us from the love of God in Christ).

Day 3
Read Psalm 63:1–8 ("I will bless you as long as I live").

Day 4
Read Ephesians 1:15–23 (the power and hope Christ offers believers).

Day 5
Read John 15:1–8 (the vine and the branches).

Day 6

Read John 15:9–17 ("I have said these things to you so that my joy may be in you, and that your joy may be complete").

Day 7

Read Psalm 118:21–29 ("Give thanks to the Lord, for he is good, for his steadfast love endures for ever").

WEEK OF PRAYER #32: LOOKING AHEAD WITH HOPE

WE CONTINUE OUR SPIRITUAL INVENTORY, but now we focus more on the future. Some questions to consider as you sift through the graces:

- How have I grown in gratitude for the gifts God has given me?
- How has my understanding of call or vocation evolved over the weeks?
- Have I made a significant decision during the retreat, or do I need God's help in making such a decision in the future?
- How would I like to structure my prayer life in the future?
- What commitments do I want to renew or make to my family, friends, church, or community? How can I better care for myself?
- How has my sensitivity to the poor and marginalized deepened over the retreat? In what concrete ways can I serve those in need?
- How have I grown in faith, hope, and love, and where does such life-giving growth lead me now? Be specific.

The Scripture suggestions for the week are intended to help you with your hope-filled praying. Rely on them to the extent they are helpful to you.

Our retreat comes to a close. As with any ending, we may experience a variety of emotions: relief, gratitude, sadness, anxiety, excitement. Be attentive to these movements and discern them well. Remember, the Spirit of God consoles, uplifts, assures, and gives us courage!

✝ Prayer for the Week

I pray for the following graces: wisdom and courage as I make and honor significant commitments; gratitude for the abundant gifts of God; zeal for the mission Christ offers me.

Day 1
Read Philippians 4:4–9 ("The peace of God, which surpasses all understanding, will guard your hearts and minds in Christ Jesus").

Day 2
Read Romans 12:9–21 (living a Christian life).

Day 3
Read James 2:14–17 ("Faith by itself, if it has no works, is dead").

Day 4
Read 1 John 4:7–21 (God is love).

Day 5
Read Colossians 3:12–17 ("Above all, clothe yourselves with love, which binds everything together in perfect harmony").

Day 6
Read Isaiah 65:17–25. Ask: *What is my vision of a "new heaven and a new earth"?*

Day 7
Read Revelation 21:1–7. Ask: *What is my dream of a "new heaven and a new earth"?*

A Prayer by Pedro Arrupe, SJ

More than ever I find myself in the hands of God.
This is what I have wanted all my life from my youth.
But now there is a difference;
the initiative is entirely with God.
It is indeed a profound spiritual experience
to know and feel myself so totally in God's hands.

PEDRO ARRUPE, SJ (1907–1991), was superior general of the Society of Jesus from 1965 to 1983, during a time of great change in the church and the world. In 1981, Arrupe suffered a stroke from which he never recovered. He wrote these words for his last address to the General Congregation of Jesuits that met in 1983 to elect his successor.

An Adventure Continues

IT WAS ASH WEDNESDAY—THE BEGINNING of the forty days of Lent—and we had journeyed into the desert. Literally.

I was spending spring break in Tucson, Arizona, on an immersion experience with a group of students from Georgetown. We were there to learn about migration on the border between the United States and Mexico. We stayed with families who had crossed the border; we visited a federal detention center that housed those held on immigration charges; and we heard the stories of people who cared for migrants during their long, arduous journey across the desert. Needless to say, there was much to soak in.

As the sun set behind the jagged mountains, we trekked across the rocky terrain to a secluded area near where we had parked. It was here, in the desert, that we had time, space, and quiet to pray about our shared experience. It was here, amid the gathering darkness, that we discussed trying to find God's light in this place and in these unlikely circumstances. It was here, in the face of all of these sobering realities, that we would celebrate Ash Wednesday.

The desert holds many layers of meaning. In the biblical stories, the desert is a place of journey; the people of Israel passed from slavery in Egypt to the Promised Land, via the wilderness. The people encountered God there. But in various traditions, the desert has been known as a dangerous place, where wild animals roam and evil spirits dwell. For Jesus, whose companions we are on this adventure, the desert was the location of growth and danger. There, he came face to face with the evil spirit who tempted him with empty promises. Like his forebears, Jesus encountered God in the wilderness, finding in that barren place confirmation of his calling and mission.

For us, too, the desert took on a heightened sense of meaning. On the border, we learned about the desert's perils by listening to heart-rending stories of people who died trying to cross it. We also met migrants who had reached the "promised land" in the United States, reuniting with family. We encountered the dynamic witness of the volunteers who ministered to migrants in the desert, bringing them water and saving them from the night-time cold.

That evening, we felt very small, overwhelmed by the human need on the border and unable to answer the myriad questions pertaining to migration.

But I encountered God that evening as we prayed together and as I recalled all the other Ash Wednesdays from my Jesuit life. Such annual rituals are like mile markers on my adventure. Looking back, I realized how itinerant my life had become. The slogan of the early Jesuits rose in my mind: "Our home is the road." But during those many years, I had not been wandering alone in the wilderness. God had been my guide, continually sending people into my life to show me the way.

I thought especially of my first Ash Wednesday as a Jesuit, which I spent in Guadalajara, Mexico. In a foreign place and culture for two months, I was out of my comfort zone and felt inadequate, disconnected from everything familiar. As these challenging weeks passed, I found myself wondering if I had what it takes to be a Jesuit.

That afternoon, as I conjugated Spanish verbs in our small Jesuit community, I saw a crowd of people walk by on the narrow street outside. Intrigued, I joined the stream of people, and we pressed into a nearby courtyard. In the middle of the crowd was a short, stout woman with graying hair. She was leading an Ash Wednesday prayer service on behalf of the local parish.

Somewhat tentatively, I approached this dignified figure. She looked into my eyes, smiled, and reached up to mark my forehead with ashes in the sign of the cross. In Spanish, she uttered the age-old formula: "Remember that you are dust, and to dust you shall return."

In the ashes, I found freedom. They told me that I do not need to be God. I do not need to have all the answers or do everything perfectly. I am a creature, a work in progress, a human being who is beautifully limited, and a sinner loved by God. The ashes connected me to all the others standing with me, marked in the same way. In our shared humanity, we discover our fragility, but also our possibility for kinship and community. We learn to rely on one another, each making up for the inadequacies of the other. In Mexico, I began to fast from perfectionism, control, and fear of the future. Marked with ashes, my fears, doubts, and self-preoccupations retreated. In their place came a deep conviction that I was where God wanted me to be.

Years later, gathered to celebrate Ash Wednesday under the Arizona sky, the ashes spoke to us all. We had learned on our immersion trip a liberating truth: we are not messiahs. We are simply called to serve others, often in small ways, and to do the best we can with the work entrusted to us. We felt that grace in the desert as each was signed with ashes. We remembered that we are dust, only human. We left room for God's grace to work in and through us. We could acknowledge to ourselves the sin and shortcomings in our lives and in our world, confident that God is not only merciful but also faithful, remaining with us.

The ashes remind us all of the ultimate beginning and end of our adventure. We are created out of love from the dust of creation, and will one day return to our Creator when God summons us home. This is not a sad thought, but a liberating reminder of who—or rather, Whose—we are most fundamentally. Our precious time on earth puts everything in perspective and instills in us a profound gratitude for the life and work we have been given and for the people God sends our way.

As a Jesuit, my adventure—symbolized in the progression from one Ash Wednesday to another—has certainly been an outward one. It has taken me to many different places. But looking more deeply at the course of my life, I appreciate how the journey has been as much interior as exterior. With the help of the Exercises and many good people, I have navigated the road from my mind to my heart. I have savored the graces that mark the Ignatian adventure—gratitude, reverence, sorrow, humility, freedom, compassion, hope, and joy—and let them come alive in my life.

Living the Spiritual Exercises

HAVING JOURNEYED THROUGH THE EXERCISES in various forms, you may wonder upon finishing them, *What do I do now?* The Exercises provided a daily and weekly structure of prayer for you. You may have enjoyed the companionship and support of a spiritual director or perhaps a group of other people making the Exercises. We are like those disciples in the upper room; we have encountered the risen Lord and have made friends in the Lord, and now we are wary about how to move forward.

Ignatius would be the first to tell us that the Exercises are not an end in themselves but a tool for the journey ahead. They are a means of finding God in all things, of deepening your relationship with Christ, of experiencing a greater interior freedom, and of discerning God's desire for you. The hope is that you have savored these graces. Over the weeks and months to come, these graces may deepen or reveal themselves in new ways, both in your prayer and in your daily living.

The Exercises are commonly called a school of prayer. You learned different ways of praying: praying with your desires, meditating on Scripture, using imagination in prayer, immersing your senses into the depth of reality, conversing with Jesus as a friend, journaling, and making the Examen daily in a spirit of gratitude. So the first and most important thing to do now is keep on praying! Ignatius insisted that the Examen is particularly important for developing a habit of discernment. To provide structure for praying with Scripture, consider praying with the daily or Sunday readings in the liturgical cycle. *Magnificat* and *Living with Christ* are two popular Catholic periodicals that contain meditations and Scripture readings for every day. Loyola Press publishes *A Book of Grace-Filled Days* for every year, also based on the lectionary readings. There are also online directories of the Sunday and daily readings.

All of us need help in our prayer: no one can make the journey of faith alone. So consider the following:

- Begin spiritual direction with a skilled director or guide.
- Join or form a faith-sharing or prayer group with others who have made the Exercises.
- Commit yourself to regular spiritual reading (a list of some suggested reading is found at the end of this book).
- Renew your commitment to be an active participant in the liturgical life of your church.

You may want to learn more about the Exercises or experience them in different forms. The reading list contains some insightful books about Ignatius and the Exercises that may further whet your spiritual appetite. Consider also making a silent, directed retreat based on the Exercises, offered by Jesuit retreat houses (for more information, see the Web site of the Society of Jesus in the United States, at http://www.jesuit.org). Some people may feel called to become a spiritual director: this is something good to talk about with an experienced director or your pastor.

In composing the Exercises, Ignatius relied on other spiritual traditions. In your prayer life, it is likewise healthy to rely on a variety of prayer forms and spiritualities. So do not limit yourself to Ignatian spirituality. Learn about other traditions.

Recall that in the Contemplation of the Love of God, which concluded the Exercises, Ignatius reminds us that love ought to show itself more by deeds than by words. Another way of living out the Exercises is by serving the needy, including those who need to hear the consoling words of the Gospel and those who suffer from poverty and injustice. Throughout the Exercises, we encountered Christ poor, and we saw how Jesus was always reaching out to those on the margins. He preached the kingdom of God to whoever would listen. Consider how you may work directly with the poor and powerless or advocate for social justice. Consider as well opportunities to serve as a catechist or liturgical minister in your parish.

Some journeys end so that others may begin. The risen Christ gave the Holy Spirit to the disciples, and the Spirit stirred up in them bold, holy desires and animated them to continue the mission that Jesus entrusted to them throughout his earthly life. The Spirit of Jesus is with us now, summoning us for the adventure ahead, as we respond ever more to the call of Christ to build a more just and gentle world where God's love reaches every nook and cranny.

When Ignatius sent his Jesuits around the globe for various missions, he would write them letters of instruction and encouragement. He often closed those letters with words intended to challenge as much as to inspire. They are fitting words to leave you with now, as you look forward to living the Exercises in your daily life:

Go and set the world on fire!

Nothing is more practical than finding God,
that is, falling in love in a quite absolute, final way.

What you are in love with,
what seizes your imagination,
will affect everything.

It will decide what will get you out of bed in the morning,
what you will do with your evenings,
how you will spend your weekends,
what you read,
whom you know,
what breaks your heart,
and what amazes you with joy and gratitude.

Fall in love,
stay in love,
and it will decide everything.

—PEDRO ARRUPE, SJ

In Gratitude

THIS GUIDE TO THE SPIRITUAL Exercises in daily life began several years ago as I directed the Exercises in different forms at Saint Joseph's University in Philadelphia and later at Holy Trinity Catholic Church and Georgetown University in Washington, D.C. I am indebted to my colleagues and students there who helped shaped this guide to its current form. Their feedback was invaluable as I tried to write a guide that would help people develop their spiritual lives, with the Ignatian tradition as an inspiration.

The Exercises are a living tradition passed on from Ignatius to men and women across the centuries. I am grateful to Gerry Blaszczak, SJ, and Howard Gray, SJ, who at different times in my Jesuit formation guided me through the thirty-day Exercises. They were faithful and wise guides, and they continue to model for me the grace of the Exercises in their lives of prayer and service. Throughout my formation as a Jesuit and now as a priest, God has blessed me with patient, astute, generous spiritual directors, including Bruce Maivelett, SJ, Jeff Chojnacki, SJ, Gordon Bennett, SJ, Paul Harman, SJ, John Haughey, SJ, and Howard Gray, SJ. In the summer of 2001, Bill Creed, SJ, and Sr. Martha Buser of the Ursuline Sisters of Louisville mentored me in giving the thirty-day retreat. Over the years that this book took shape, I was able to rely on the support, friendship, encouragement, and good advice of George Witt, SJ, Kurt Denk, SJ, Steve Spahn, SJ, Jeanne Ruesch, Catherine Heinhold, Sister Helen Scarry, RJM, Kathleen Looney, Martina O'Shea, Matt Carnes, SJ, Phil Boroughs, SJ, Tim Brown, SJ, and Jim Shea, SJ. By word and example, each of these sons and daughters of Ignatius kindled in me a devotion to Christ; a passion for the ministry of the Exercises; and a zeal to "help souls," as Ignatius often said.

I am indebted to James Martin, SJ, and Brian McDermott, SJ, for taking the time to review the completed manuscript of this book and offering their fraternal encouragement. And to Tim

O'Brien, SJ, who so carefully edited the text, checked references, and offered me fresh insights for the first draft of the manuscript to the very last one. I am grateful in particular for his contributions to the explanatory text for the Contemplation of the Love of God. I am confident that you will be reading one of his books one day soon. Finally, my thanks to Vinita Wright and Joe Durepos from Loyola Press who helped bring this book to birth after many years of labor.

To many goes the credit, but to God always goes the glory.

Acknowledgments

FOR THE SUMMARY OF IGNATIUS'S LIFE I relied on Ignatius's auto-biography, dictated to Luis Gonçalves da Câmara, in Joseph N. Tylenda, SJ, *A Pilgrim's Journey: The Autobiography of Ignatius of Loyola* (Collegeville, MN: Liturgical Press, 1991). Also of help were John W. O'Malley, SJ, *The First Jesuits* (Cambridge, MA: Harvard University Press, 1993), and biographical sketches written by John J. Callahan, SJ, for Marquette University faculty and Norman O'Neale, SJ, written for Jesuit High in New Orleans.

For **direct quotations from the Exercises** I have chosen the translation of George E. Ganss, SJ, in *The Spiritual Exercises of Saint Ignatius* (St. Louis: Institute of Jesuit Sources, 1992). I recognize that some of the language may be off-putting to modern readers, especially masculine references to God and militaristic and feudal imagery. However, I believe that it is important for today's pray-ers to access Ignatius's text (and thus his mind and heart) as directly as possible. At different points in the Exercises, I refer readers to the contemporary translation offered by David L. Fleming, SJ, in *Draw Me into Your Friendship: The Spiritual Exercises—A Literal Translation and a Contemporary Reading* (St. Louis: Institute of Jesuit Sources, 1996).

In crafting my **commentary** that introduces the prayer for each week, I relied on the following: George A. Aschenbrenner, SJ, *Stretched for Greater Glory: What to Expect from the Spiritual Exercises* (Chicago: Loyola Press, 2004); William A Barry, SJ, *Letting God Come Close: An Approach to the Ignatian Spiritual Exercises* (Chicago: Loyola Press, 2001); Dean Brackley, SJ, *The Call to Discernment in Troubled Times: New Perspectives on the Transformative Wisdom of Ignatius of Loyola* (New York: Crossroad Publishing, 2004); Michael Ivens, SJ, *Understanding the Spiritual Exercises: Text and Commentary* (Herefordshire, UK: Gracewing, 1998); Joseph A. Tetlow, SJ, *Making Choices in Christ: The Foundations of Ignatian Spirituality* (Chicago: Loyola Press, 2008); and Fr. Ganss's endnotes to his translation of the Exercises (cited earlier). My living commentary on the Exercises was provided by the spiritual directors with whom I have made retreats over my years as a Jesuit. I acknowledge in particular Gerry Blaszczak, SJ, and Howard Gray, SJ, who at different times in my Jesuit life so graciously and wisely guided me through the thirty-day retreat. My words are in many places reflections of what I learned from them during those retreats

For my commentary on the **discernment of spirits** I relied on the sources mentioned here and on the clear and concise exposition of the rules by Timothy M. Gallagher, OMV, in *The Discernment of Spirits: An Ignatian Guide for Everyday Living* (New York: Crossroad Publishing, 2005), and *Spiritual Consolation: An Ignatian Guide for the Greater Discernment of Spirits* (New York: Crossroad, 2007).

There are many different versions of the **nineteenth-annotation retreat** available to today's pray-ers. In constructing the daily and weekly plan for this retreat, I consulted the following sources: James W. Skehan, SJ, *Place Me with Your Son: Ignatian Spirituality in Everyday Life*, 3rd ed. (Washington, D.C.: Georgetown University Press, 1991); Carol Ann Smith, SHCJ, and Eugene F. Merz, SJ, *Moment by Moment: A Retreat in Everyday Life* (Notre Dame, IN: Ave Maria Press, 2000); Joseph Tetlow, SJ, *Choosing Christ in the World: Directing the Spiritual Exercises of St. Ignatius Loyola according to Annotations Eighteen and Nineteen* (St. Louis: Institute of Jesuit Sources, 1989); and John A. Veltri, SJ, *Orientations*, vol. 2 (Guelph, ON: Guelph Centre of Spirituality, 1998). I owe to Veltri the inspiration to divide the Exercises into weeks of prayer, with Scripture or other meditations for each day of the week. I also rely on Veltri's authority to move the Contemplation on the Call of Christ, our King, from its traditional place at the opening of the Second Week of the Exercises to its place in this book, after the Contemplations on the Incarnation, the Nativity, and the Hidden Life.

Scripture texts are taken from the New Revised Standard Version translation, in the *HarperCollins Bible* (New York: HarperCollins Publishers, 1993).

Sources

Page 6: Quote from Joseph N. Tylenda, trans. *A Pilgrim's Journey: The Autobiography of Ignatius of Loyola* (San Francisco: Ignatius Press, 2001), 48.

Page 8: Quote from Joseph N. Tylenda, trans. *A Pilgrim's Journey: The Autobiography of Ignatius of Loyola* (San Francisco: Ignatius Press, 2001), 104.

Page 37: A Prayer by Thomas Merton from *Thoughts in Solitude* (New York: Farrar, Straus, & Cudahy, 1958), 83.

Page 41: *Anima Christi* traditional translation by George E. Ganss, in *The Spiritual Exercises of Saint Ignatius* (St. Louis: Institute of Jesuit Sources, 1992), 20.

Page 42: *Anima Christi* contemporary translation by David Fleming, in *Hearts on Fire: Praying with Jesuits*, Michael Harter, ed. (Chicago: Loyola Press, 2004), 3.

Page 47: "Messenger" from Mary Oliver, *Thirst* (Boston: Beacon Press, 2006), 1.

Page 48: "Prayer, understood as the distilled awareness . . ." from James Finley, ed., *Merton's Palace of Nowhere* (Notre Dame, IN: Ave Maria Press, 1978), 32.

Page 48: "Prayer has far more to do with what God wants . . ." from Ruth Burrows, *Essence of Prayer* (Mahwah, NJ: Paulist Press, 2006), 176.

Page 51: The Saints Speak to Us about Prayer, various quotes from *United States Catholic Catechism for Adults* (Washington, DC: United States Conference of Catholic Bishops, 2006), 463, 479, 480.

Page 62: A Prayer by St. Anselm of Canterbury, traditional prayer quoted in William A. Barry, *A Friendship Like No Other:*

Experiencing God's Amazing Embrace (Chicago: Loyola Press, 2008), xix.

Page 67: Principle and Foundation: Traditional Translation from George E. Ganss, *The Spiritual Exercises of Saint Ignatius* (St. Louis: Institute of Jesuit Sources, 1992), 32.

Page 69: Principle and Foundation: Contemporary Translation from David L. Fleming, *Draw Me into Your Friendship: The Spiritual Exercises—A Literal Translation and a Contemporary Reading* (St. Louis: Institute of Jesuit Sources, 1996), 27.

Page 70: "It is true to say that for me . . ." from Thomas Merton, *New Seeds of Contemplation* (New York: New Directions, 1972), 31.

Page 73: "Praying" from Mary Oliver, *Thirst* (Boston: Beacon Press), 37.

Page 73: A Prayer by John Henry Newman from *Meditations and Devotions of the Late Cardinal Newman* (New York: Longmans, Green, and Co., 1893), 301.

Page 88: A Prayer by Pierre Teilhard de Chardin, SJ, *Ad Majorem Dei Gloriam: A Collection of Prayers, Pictures and Poems for Friends of the Jesuits* (Oregon Province Jesuit Seminary and Mission Bureau, 1979).

Page 96: "Prayer is a matter of relationship." From William A. Barry, *Letting God Come Close: An Approach to the Ignatian Spiritual Exercises* (Chicago: Loyola Press, 2001), 55.

Page 101: "He who goes about to reform the world . . ." from Patrick J. Ryan, ed., *Thoughts of St. Ignatius Loyola for Every Day of the Year* (New York: Fordham University Press, 2006), 74.

Page 107: A Prayer by Karl Rahner from Albert Raffelt, ed., *Karl Rahner: Prayers for a Lifetime* (New York: Crossroad, 1984), 8.

Page 114: "If you want to make progress in love . . ." from Patrick J. Ryan, ed., *Thoughts of St. Ignatius Loyola for Every Day of the Year* (New York: Fordham University Press, 2006), 82.

Page 115: Quote from Joseph N. Tylenda, ed., *A Pilgrim's Journey: The Autobiography of Ignatius of Loyola* (San Francisco: Ignatius Press, 2001), 48.

Page 127: A Prayer for Oscar Romero and Other Departed Priests. Office of Justice, Peace and integrity of Creation (JPIC) Congregation of Notre Dame. www.jpic-visitation.org/reflec tions/prayers/romero.html

Page 132: "Undertake nothing without consulting God" from Patrick J. Ryan, ed., *Thoughts of St. Ignatius Loyola for Every Day of the Year* (New York: Fordham University Press, 2006), 106.

Page 133: "Consider a blissfully happy couple . . ." from Ruth Burrows, *Essence of Prayer* (Mahwah, NJ: HiddenSpring, 2006), 74.

Page 158: "It is not the critic who counts . . ." from Louis Auchincloss, ed., *Theodore Roosevelt: Letters and Speeches* (New York: The Library of America, 2004), 181–2.

Page 161: A Loving Disciple's Offering from Joseph Tetlow, *Choosing Christ in the World* (St. Louis: The Institute of Jesuit Sources, 1989), 49.

Page 164: "The laborers in the Lord's vineyard . . ." from Patrick J. Ryan, ed., *Thoughts of St. Ignatius Loyola for Every Day of the Year* (New York: Fordham University Press, 2006), 25.

Page 174: "Solidarity is the social meaning of humility. . . ." from Dean Brackley, *The Call to Discernment in Troubled Times* (New York: Crossroad, 2004), 100–101.

Page 180: "The entire life of a good Christian . . ." from St. Augustine, quoted in Peter van Breemen, *The God Who Won't Let Go* (Notre Dame, IN: Ave Maria Press, 2001), 147–148.

Page 187: "The saint is unlike everybody else . . ." and "A humble man is not disturbed" from Thomas Merton, *New Seeds of Contemplation* (New York: New Directions, 1972), 99, 188.

Page 196: "It is the Kingdom of love, justice, and mercy . . ." from the *United States Catholic Catechism for Adults* (Washington, DC: United States Conference of Catholic Bishops, 2006), 486.

Page 199: A Prayer by St. Teresa of Ávila; these words were on a slip of paper in her prayer book at the time of her death. This is one of various translations.

Page 202: St. Ignatius's Prayer for Generosity. As cited in John A. Mullin, *Stay with Us: Praying as Disciples* (Williston Park, NY: Resurrection Press, 1995).

Page 207: For Further Reflection material from Michael J. Himes, *The Mystery of Faith* (Cincinnati: St. Anthony Messenger, 2004), chapter 3.

Page 215: "Lord, make me an instrument of your peace" as cited in John A. Mullin, *Stay with Us: Praying as Disciples* (Williston Park, NY: Resurrection Press, 1995).

Page 218: Quote from Michael Harter, ed., *Hearts on Fire: Praying with Jesuits* (Chicago: Loyola Press, 2004), 117.

Page 224: "You ask whether your verses are good" from Rainer Maria Rilke, *Letters to a Young Poet* (New York: W.W. Norton and Co., 1963), 18–19.

Page 229: Colloquy before Christ Crucified: Contemporary Translation from David L. Fleming, *Draw Me into Your Friendship: The Spiritual Exercises—A Literal Translation and a Contemporary Reading* (St. Louis: Institute of Jesuit Sources, 1996), 49.

Page 232: quotes from Michael Harter, ed., *Hearts on Fire: Praying with Jesuits* (Chicago: Loyola Press, 2004), 134, 111.

Page 243: "We will never win the Olympics of humanity . . ." from Friends of L'Arche Atlanta, www.friendsoflarcheatlanta.org/what.html

Page 247: "In the final analysis, talking about prayer doesn't matter . . ." Karl Rahner, *The Need and the Blessing of Prayer*, trans. Bruce W. Gillette (Collegeville, MN: The Order of St. Benedict, Inc, 1997), 101.

Page 254: "Lord, you have made us for Yourself . . ." from St. Augustine, *Confessions, Book 1* as translated by F.J. Sheed (Indianapolis, IN: Hackett, 1993) and R.S. Pine-Coffin (New York: Penguin, 1961).

Page 254: "The day will come when . . ." from Pierre Teihlard de Chardin, *Toward the Future*, Rene Hague trans. (New York: Harcourt Brace Jovanovich, 1975), 86–87.

Page 255: A Prayer by Rabindranath Tagore from *The Heart of God: Prayers of Rabindranath Tagore* (Boston: Tuttle Publishing, 1997), 44.

Page 258: A Prayer by St. Teresa of Ávila is traditionally attributed to her. This prayer is found in various sources but appears here as cited in John A. Mullin, *Stay with Us: Praying as Disciples* (Williston Park, NY: Resurrection Press, 1995).

Page 264: A Prayer by Pedro Arrupe, SJ, from Documents of the 33rd General Congregation of the Society of Jesus, September 1983.

Page 272: "Nothing is more practical than finding God . . ." from www.jesuitswisprov.org/spirituality_main.php

Spiritual Resources for the Journey of Faith

Prayer in General and How to Pray

Barry, William A., SJ. *A Friendship Like No Other: Experiencing God's Amazing Embrace*. Chicago: Loyola Press, 2008.

———. *With an Everlasting Love: Developing an Intimate Relationship with God*. New York: Paulist Press, 1999.

———. *God and You: Prayer as a Personal Relationship*. New York: Paulist Press, 1987.

Green, Thomas H., SJ. *Opening to God: A Guide to Prayer*. Rev. ed. Notre Dame, IN: Ave Maria Press, 2006.

———. *Weeds among the Wheat: Discernment, Where Prayer and Action Meet*. Notre Dame, IN: Ave Maria Press, 1984.

———. *When the Well Runs Dry: Prayer beyond the Beginnings*. Rev. ed. Notre Dame, IN: Ave Maria Press, 2007.

Langford, Jeremy. *Seeds of Faith: Practices to Grow a Healthy Spiritual Life*. Brewster, MA: Paraclete Press, 2007.

Oliva, Max, SJ. *Free to Pray, Free to Love: Growing in Prayer and Compassion*. Notre Dame, IN: Ave Maria Press, 1994.

Rupp, Joyce. *Prayer*. Maryknoll, NY: Orbis Books, 2007.

Thibodeaux, Mark E., SJ. *Armchair Mystic: Easing into Contemplative Prayer*. Cincinnati: St. Anthony Messenger Press, 2001.

———. *God, I Have Issues: 50 Ways to Pray No Matter How You Feel*. Cincinnati, OH: St. Anthony Messenger Press, 2005.

Spiritual Exercises in General

Aschenbrenner, George A., SJ. *Stretched for Greater Glory: What to Expect from the Spiritual Exercises*. Chicago: Loyola Press, 2004.

Barry, William A., SJ. *Finding God in All Things: A Companion to the Spiritual Exercises of St. Ignatius*. Notre Dame, IN: Ave Maria Press, 1991.

———. *Letting God Come Close: An Approach to the Ignatian Spiritual Exercises*. Chicago: Loyola Press, 2001.

Brackley, Dean, SJ. *The Call to Discernment in Troubled Times: New Perspectives on the Transformative Wisdom of Ignatius of Loyola*. New York: Crossroad Publishing, 2004.

Dyckman, Katherine, Mary Garvin, and Elizabeth Liebert. *The Spiritual Exercises Reclaimed: Uncovering Liberating Possibilities for Women*. New York: Paulist Press, 2001.

English, John J., SJ. *Spiritual Freedom: From an Experience of the Ignatian Exercises to the Art of Spiritual Guidance*. 2nd ed. Chicago: Loyola Press, 1995.

Fagin, Gerald, SJ. *Putting on the Heart of Christ: How the Spiritual Exercises Invite Us to a Virtuous Life*. Chicago: Loyola Press, 2010.

Fleming, David L., SJ. *What Is Ignatian Spirituality?* Chicago: Loyola Press, 2008.

Gallagher, Timothy M., OMV. *The Discernment of Spirits: An Ignatian Guide for Everyday Living*. New York: Crossroad Publishing, 2005.

———. *Spiritual Consolation: An Ignatian Guide for the Greater Discernment of Spirits*. New York: Crossroad Publishing, 2007.

Lonsdale, David. *Eyes to See, Ears to Hear: An Introduction to Ignatian Spirituality*. Maryknoll, NY: Orbis Books, 2000.

———. *Listening to the Music of the Spirit: the Art of Discernment.* Notre Dame, IN: Ave Maria Press, 1992.

Silf, Margaret. *Inner Compass: An Invitation to Ignatian Spirituality.* Chicago: Loyola Press, 1999.

Sparough, J. Michael, SJ, Jim Manney, and Tim Hipskind, SJ. *What's Your Decision: How to Make Choices with Confidence and Clarity.* Chicago: Loyola Press, 2010.

Tetlow, Joseph A., SJ. *Making Choices in Christ: The Foundations of Ignatian Spirituality.* Chicago: Loyola Press, 2008.

Thibodeaux, Mark E., SJ. *God's Voice Within: The Ignatian Way to Discover God's Will.* Chicago: Loyola Press, 2010.

Jesuits and Jesuit History

Barry, William A., SJ, and Robert Doherty, SJ. *Contemplatives in Action: The Jesuit Way.* New York: Paulist Press, 2002.

Boyle, Gregory, SJ *Tattoos on the Heart: The Power of Boundless Compassion.* New York: Free Press, 2010.

Burke, Kevin, SJ. *Pedro Arrupe: Essential Writings.* Maryknoll, NY: Orbis Books, 2004.

Burke, Kevin, SJ, and Eileen Burke Sullivan. *The Ignatian Tradition.* Collegeville, MN: Liturgical Press, 2009.

Byron, William J., SJ. *Jesuit Saturdays: Sharing the Ignatian Spirit with Lay Colleagues and Friends.* Chicago: Loyola Press, 2000.

Lowney, Chris. *Heroic Leadership: Best Practices from a 450-Year-Old Company that Changed the World.* Chicago: Loyola Press, 2003.

———. *Heroic Living: Discover Your Purpose and Change the World.* Chicago: Loyola Press, 2009.

Martin, James, SJ. *In Good Company: The Fast Track from the Corporate World to Poverty, Chastity and Obedience.* Franklin, WI: Sheed and Ward, 2000.

———. *The Jesuit Guide to Almost Everything: A Spirituality for Real Life.* New York: Harper Collins, 2010.

Modras, Ronald. *Ignatian Humanism: A Dynamic Spirituality for the 21st Century.* Chicago: Loyola Press, 2004.

O'Malley, John W., SJ. *The First Jesuits.* Cambridge, MA: Harvard University Press, 1993.

Smith, Gary, SJ. *Radical Compassion: Finding Christ in the Heart of the Poor.* Chicago: Loyola Press, 2002.

———. *They Come Back Singing: Finding God with the Refugees.* Chicago: Loyola Press, 2008.

Tylenda, Joseph N., SJ. *A Pilgrim's Journey: the Autobiography of Ignatius of Loyola.* Collegeville, MN: Liturgical Press, 1985.

Prayer Exercises and Guides

Alexander, Andy, SJ, Maureen Waldron, and Larry Gillick, SJ. *Retreat in the Real World: Finding Intimacy with God Wherever You Are.* Chicago: Loyola Press, 2009.

Bergan, Jacqueline, and Marie Schwan. *Praying with Ignatius of Loyola.* Winona, MN: Saint Mary's Press, 1991.

Daly, Michael J., and Lee P. Yerzell. *In All Things: Everyday Prayers of Jesuit High School Students.* Chicago: Loyola Press, 2003.

De Mello, Anthony, SJ. *The Way to Love: The Last Meditations of Anthony De Mello.* New York: Doubleday, 1991.

———. *Sadhana, A Way to God: Christian Exercises in Eastern Form.* New York: Doubleday, 1978.

————. *Wellsprings: A Book of Spiritual Exercises*. New York: Doubleday, 1984.

Harter, Michael, SJ. *Hearts on Fire: Praying with Jesuits*. St. Louis: Institute of Jesuit Sources, 1993.

Manney, Jim. *A Simple, Life-Changing Prayer*, Chicago: Loyola Press, 2011.

Merrill, Nan C. *Psalms for Praying: An Invitation to Wholeness*. 2nd ed. New York: Continuum, 2006.

Muldoon, Tim. *The Ignatian Workout: Daily Spiritual Exercises for a Healthy Faith*. Chicago: Loyola Press, 2004.

O'Malley, William, SJ. *Daily Prayers for Busy People*. Ligouri, MO: Ligouri Publications, 2003.

————. *More Daily Prayers for Busy People*. Ligouri, MO: Ligouri Publications, 2003.

Smith, Carol Ann, SHCJ, and Eugene Merz, SJ. *Moment by Moment: A Retreat in Everyday Life*. Notre Dame, IN: Ave Maria Press, 2000.

Thibodeaux, Mark. *Reimagining the Ignatian Examen*. Chicago: Loyola Press, 2015

Wright, Vinita Hampton. *Days of Deepening Friendship: For the Woman Who Wants Authentic Life with God*. Chicago: Loyola Press, 2009.

Spiritual Reading

Barry, William A., SJ. *A Friendship Like No Other: Experiencing God's Amazing Embrace*. Chicago: Loyola Press, 2008.

Benedict XVI. *Saved in Hope*. San Francisco: Ignatius Press, 2008.

Bernardin, Joseph Cardinal. *The Gift of Peace*. Chicago: Loyola Press, 1997.

Ciszek, Walter J., SJ. *He Leadeth Me*. San Francisco: Ignatius Press, 1995.

John Paul II. *Crossing the Threshold of Hope*. New York: Albert A. Knopf, 1995.

Lamott, Anne. *Traveling Mercies: Some Thoughts on Faith*. New York: Random House, 2000.

Martin, James, SJ. *The Jesuit Guide to Almost Everything: A Spirituality for Real Life*. New York: HarperCollins, 2010.

——. *My Life with the Saints*. Chicago: Loyola Press, 2006.

Metz, Johannes Baptist. *Poverty of Spirit*. New York: Paulist Press, 1998.

Mother Teresa. *A Simple Path*. New York: Random House, 1995.

Muller, Wayne. *Sabbath: Finding Rest, Renewal, and Delight in Our Busy Lives*. New York: Random House, 1999.

Norris, Kathleen. *Amazing Grace: A Vocabulary of Faith*. New York: Penguin, 1999.

Nouwen, Henri J. *Life of the Beloved: Spiritual Living in the Secular World*. New York: Crossroad Publishing, 2002.

——. *The Return of the Prodigal Son: A Story of Homecoming*. New York: Doubleday, 1992.

Rahner, Karl, SJ. *Encounters with Silence*. South Bend, IN: St. Augustine's Press, 1999.

——. *The Need and Blessing of Prayer*. Collegeville, MN: Liturgical Press, 1997.

Radcliffe, Timothy. *Why Go to Church: The Drama of the Eucharist*. New York: Continuum, 2008.

Rolheiser, Ronald. *The Holy Longing: The Search for a Christian Spirituality.* New York: Doubleday, 1999.

———. *The Restless Heart: Finding Our Spiritual Home in Times of Loneliness.* New York: Doubleday, 2004.

van Breemen, Peter. *The God Who Won't Let Go.* Notre Dame, IN: Ave Maria Press, 2001.

Vanier, Jean. *Befriending the Stranger.* Grand Rapids, MI: Eerdmans Publishing, 2005.

Online Prayer Resources

The following sites offer interactive prayer exercises and retreats:

Creighton University Online Ministries
http://www.creighton.edu/CollaborativeMinistry/online.html

Daily Prayer Online
http://www.pray.com.au

Finding God Program Resources,
http://www.findinggod.org

IgnatianSpirtuality.com
http://www.IgnatianSpirituality.com

Where Will You Find God Today?,
http://www.loyolapress.com/other6.aspx

Pray-as-You-Go.org: Daily Prayer for Your MP3 Player
http://www.pray-as-you-go.org

Sacred Space: Daily Prayer Online
http://www.sacredspace.ie

Other helpful sites:

Jesuit Collaborative (various resources for giving the
Spiritual Exercises)
http://www.jesuit-collaborative.org

The Society of Jesus in the United States,
http://www.jesuit.org

New American Bible Online
http://www.usccb.org/nab

Busted Halo
http://www.bustedhalo.com

A.M.D.G.
Ad Majorem Dei Gloriam
"For the Greater Glory of God"